REYNOLDS PRICE

A *Bibliography*
1949–1984

REYNOLDS PRICE
A *Bibliography*
1949–1984

Stuart Wright
and
James L. W. West III

PUBLISHED FOR THE BIBLIOGRAPHICAL SOCIETY
OF THE UNIVERSITY OF VIRGINIA
BY THE UNIVERSITY PRESS OF VIRGINIA
CHARLOTTESVILLE

A Linton R. Massey Descriptive Bibliography

THE UNIVERSITY PRESS OF VIRGINIA
Copyright © 1986 by the Rector and Visitors
of the University of Virginia

First published 1986

Frontispiece: self-portrait by Reynolds Price.

Library of Congress Cataloging-in-Publication Data
Wright, Stuart T.
Reynolds Price : a bibliography, 1949–1984.

"A Linton R. Massey descriptive bibliography"—T.p. verso.
Includes index.
1. Price, Reynolds, 1933–   —Bibliography.
I. West, James L. W.   II. University of Virginia.
Bibliographical Society.   III. Title.
Z8713.43.W75   1986   [PS3566.R54]   016.813'54   85-29463
ISBN 0-8139-1092-7

Printed in the United States of America

Contents

Foreword

When I began writing in earnest at the age of eleven or twelve, I assumed that I was speaking to and for someone. My first substantial effort, after the assigned verse of primary school, was a play—the most public of forms (and a play about the birth of Jesus, not exactly a marooned preadolescent). The someone was a teacher I'd fallen in love with that year, as I did most years, and the few relatives and classmates who knew of my effort. At the time I thought they were sufficient audience. I hadn't imagined hordes of the famished buying my wisdom.

Just as well. For while I've been mostly lucky in the reception of my adult work, I've come to see that my childhood aim was accurate. I've even come to believe more than half the time that in western culture, in any known century, there has been a mystically determined number of serious readers—larger maybe than the fixed number of Just Men but an absolute not a relative quantity for each society. I suspect for instance that Homer had, head for head, as many serious listeners in the eighth century B.C. as Bernard Malamud or Katherine Anne Porter in America today—fewer than five thousand certainly.

I'm not speaking of sales figures or the number of eyes that traverse a particular work. Manipulated by ads, reviews, and self-fulfilling bestseller charts, the number of sold copies of a serious book is meaningless to anyone but accountants. I'm speaking of readers who actually meet a book with resources equivalent to its own—time, sympathy, intelligence, indifference to fashion. All good books find them eventually, and their response is a writer's second-largest reward.

The largest is the work itself. Good writers, like other good artists, are finally working for themselves and maybe some numinous judge— and working from the necessity to exercise a faculty, an intangible organ but one as *given* and demanding as a liver or pancreas. The primacy of that exercise explains why many writers are careless of reputation or even of the occasional Just Reader. As rattled as writers can be, in the short run, by reviews or the vicissitudes of publishing, they ultimately rest (or fall exhausted) upon a few artifacts—a row of stories or poems. That's the paradox of their lives, speaking to be heard but at least accepting the speech itself as its own suspended end.

Which is not to say that even the most philosophic of writers—Shakespeare, Dickinson, Kafka—are not susceptible to surprise and gratitude at various kinds of attention, from baked goods to propositions. Only that the attentions come from a world quite different from the one addressed. For their passionate witness and report, they receive intermittent ministry in an almost indecipherable language.

It's likely in fact that there have always been more good ministers to writers than there have been good readers, though the two categories are not mutually exclusive. Bankrollers, printers, biographers (there your writer must be dead), textual detectives, the immensely rare good critic, the bibliographer—even a curmudgeon is secretly grateful to them all. But the single necessity is the bibliographer. Without his meticulous hunt, his public list, no really adequate response to a prolific writer can hope to begin.

Children honor lists. They instinctively know their value as guides and comforts when waiting. As a grade-school writer I poured out lists like oil on the breakers—"The People I Love," "People Who Might Love Me," "Movies I Have Seen," "Great People I Have Seen or Touched" (Franklin Roosevelt, General Eisenhower, Marian Anderson), "Books I Will Write." Nearly forty years later here's an external list—"What He's Managed till Now."

What it will mean to anyone but me, I can't easily guess. Only an abjectly Just Reader will track down more than a few of the strays spotted here, and I wince at owning up to my righteous editorials for the high-school newspaper or the early book reviews in which I thought I was licensed to do a little turn of my own on a prostrate author or the interviews in which I rattled away (and got the misquotation I deserved). But the boy who unknowingly began a life's work with "The Wise Men" in 1946 is still alarmingly at large in the man who writes this; and they both are mainly pleased—a long careful list, a proof at least of time *spent*, a dare to augment it.

REYNOLDS PRICE

Acknowledgments

We are especially grateful to Reynolds Price for his interest and cooperation. We also thank John L. Sharpe III, Curator of Rare Books, and Mattie Russell, Curator of Manuscripts, Perkins Library, Duke University, for providing access to their extensive collections of Price materials. We thank H. Gordon Bechanan, former Director of Libraries, and Charles W. Haney, Assistant Humanities Librarian, Newman Library, VPI&SU, for building a large and useful Price collection. Mary Larimer and Beverly Massengill, both formerly of the Special Collections Department at the Newman Library, were also most helpful. Rare book dealer Bradford Morrow was instrumental in helping the Newman Library acquire its Price materials. Clayton S. Owens of Winthrop College Library was Price's first bibliographer; his listings have provided a useful beginning point for our own work.[1]

George Bixby of Ampersand Books provided information about the Price publications with Albondocani Press and was kind enough to read a draft of Section A of the bibliography and to make useful suggestions to West. Harry Ford of Atheneum provided information about Price's books and press runs. Thanks are also due the following persons for various kinds of assistance: Jeffrey Anderson, Anne S. Carter (NAL), John M. Clum, Anne M. Davidson (Chatto & Windus), Laird Ellis, Emma Glover (Arlington Books), Bruce High, Roger Highfield, Howard Jones, Allene Keith, Dr. Gene Lanier, Gary M. Lepper, E. R. Loessin, W. U. McDonald, Jr., Stathis Orphanos, Phyllis Peacock, Sam Ragan, John Rolfe (Penguin), Joanne Sharpe, Jack Shoemaker, Francis Law Sullivan, Ralph Sylvester, G. Thomas Tanselle, Mr. J. Trindade, Synnove Vervik, A. S. Wendel, and J. Howard Woolmer. Special thanks to Nancy Clausen for compiling the index.

1. Owens, "Reynolds Price: A Bibliography," M.A. thesis, Univ. of North Carolina, Chapel Hill, 1976. Owens also prepared the Price entry in vol. I of *First Printings of American Authors* (Detroit: Gale Research Co., 1977), pp. 301–3. A useful list of A and B items is Ray A. Roberts, "Reynolds Price: A Bibliographical Checklist," *American Book Collector*, July–August 1981, pp. 15–23.

Bibliographical Method

This bibliography lists and describes the known publications of American novelist Reynolds Price. It is a record of his literary career to date, intended primarily for scholars and collectors interested in his writings. For each of Price's books this bibliography includes a description of the first impression of the first American edition. The descriptive formularies are taken from Fredson Bowers, *Principles of Bibliographical Description* (Princeton: Princeton University Press, 1949), with modifications from G. Thomas Tanselle and further modifications by West. Descriptions for each book contain paragraphs for title page, copyright page, dedication page (when present), collation, contents, running titles (when present), typography, paper, binding or casing, and jacket or wrappers. All measurements are recorded in millimeters. All words hyphenated between lines in quasi-facsimiles are to be read as one word.

Title Page: Title pages are quasi-facsimiled, with ink colors given in square brackets. Once a color is given, all subsequent lines are in that color until another color is given. Unless otherwise indicated, all printing is in black ink.

Copyright and *Dedication Pages*: These pages are quasi-facsimiled.

Collation: The standard Bowers formulary is used with three changes: there is no indication of format (8°, 16°), dimensions of the page are not enclosed within parentheses, and the number of leaves is not given.

Contents: Standard Bowers formularies are again used; there is, however, no abbreviation "p." or "pp." for "page" or "pages," and descriptions of each page or section are followed by semicolons rather than by periods.

Signatures: All books described in this bibliography have unsigned gatherings; therefore no paragraphs for signatures are included.

Running Titles: The location of the running title on the type page is given first. Then the printing is quasi-facsimiled from the left margin of the verso page across the gutter to the right margin of the recto page. A single vertical bar stands for the gutter. Foliation is not noted.

Typography: Here the method is adapted from Tanselle's "The Identification of Type Faces in Bibliographical Description," *PBSA*, 60 (1966), 185–202. No attempt is made to identify type families or faces.

Paper: Tanselle's "The Bibliographical Description of Paper," *SB*, 24 (1971), 26–67, serves as the guide. Sheet size and bulking measurement are not given.

Binding or *Casing*: These paragraphs are based on Tanselle's "The Bibliographical Description of Patterns," *SB*, 23 (1970), 71–102. Cloth patterns are described verbally; stamping is quasi-facsimiled; edges, endpapers, and bands (when present) are described.

Jacket or *Wrappers*: Descriptions here are patterned after those in Tanselle's "Book-Jackets, Blurbs, and Bibliographers," *Library*, 5th ser., 26 (June 1971), 91–134.

Notes: The first note for each title gives publication date, retail price, and press run of the first impression. The next note, in descriptions of limited signed editions and broadsides, presents a quasi-facsimile of the statement of limitation. Other notes deal with later American impressions, British publication, and oddities of binding or manufacture. Advance copies are described in detail when exemplars have been available to the compilers. In several cases no copy has been seen, and the notes are based on limited descriptions provided by Price collectors. With one exception (**A3b**), all American paperback editions of Price's books have been published by Avon Books. Inquiries to this publisher about press runs and precise publication dates have gone unanswered, and we have therefore had to rely, for publication dates, on information printed on the copyright pages of the editions themselves. For press runs we are unable to supply data.

The system of labeling should be explained. Each section of this bibliography is designated by a letter, and each title within a section bears an arabic numeral. Thus all entries for Price's first book, *A Long and Happy Life*, begin with **A1**. Separate *editions* (i.e., fresh typesettings) are indicated by lower-case letters. The first edition of *A Long and Happy Life* is therefore **A1a**, the second edition **A1b**, and so forth. No label designations are given for *plating, impression, issue,* or *state*. All clothbound impressions are mentioned; all editions subsequent to the first are noted but not described.[1]

---

1. For a definition of the term *plating* and some examples of its possible uses, see West, "The Bibliographical Concept of *Plating*," *SB*, 36 (1983), 252–66.

No textual collations have been performed. Price has occasionally ordered plate changes in later impressions of his books, but these changes have always been corrections of demonstrable errors. Price does not have true revisions introduced into the plates of his books, nor does he revise from edition to edition as, for example, his contemporary John Barth does. Price feels that such revising would be improper, since he would in effect be another person—older and with altered perceptions—revising the work of a younger and considerably different version of himself. Price does remember that he had minor plate changes made for the second impressions of A *Long and Happy Life*, *The Names and Faces of Heroes*, and *The Surface of Earth*. Price also recalls making revisions for the Avon paperback edition of *The Surface of Earth* in order to adjust the chronology of the novel.

The descriptions in Section A are based on examination of copies in four Price collections: (1) the collection in the Rare Books Department, Perkins Library, Duke University, which contains materials placed there by Price and by William Blackburn, his teacher at Duke; (2) the collection at the Newman Library, Virginia Polytechnic Institute and State University; (3) Wright's personal collection; and (4) Price's personal collection. No record of individual copies examined is included in this bibliography.

Separately bound offprints of appearances in periodicals are not described as "A" items in this bibliography. To do so would dignify offprints beyond their significance and would be out of keeping with the circumstances and intent of their publication. Offprints are therefore noted with individual entries in Sections C–E.

Section B of this bibliography lists two kinds of "B" items: previously unpublished contributions to books (those items which appear for the first time ever as book contributions) and first book appearances (items which have appeared first in another publication—usually a periodical—and are being republished in a collection by divers hands for the first time). These two kinds of "B" items are differentiated from one another by notes following the citations in the entries. Any further republications of the latter kind of item are listed in Section C following the citations to the original periodical appearances.[2]

Section C is a listing of appearances in periodicals and newspapers. The annotations and quotations here are particularly full—especially for the juvenilia, which is not easily accessible. Section D is a listing of translations, by title, with brief descriptions of pagination and binding. Section E is a record of interviews, published discussions, and published comments. This material is often quite useful to the scholar or critic, and Wright has cast a wide net. Annotations are again generous in length so that the user of this bibliography can locate easily what he is seeking and bypass what will be of little value to him.

This bibliography has been an equal collaboration. Wright provided

2. See West, "Section B and the Bibliographer," *Analytical and Enumerative Bibliography*, 7 (1983), 31–36.

the initial impetus for the project: he is responsible for Sections B, C, E, and F. West has compiled Sections A and D; he has also written this description of the bibliographical method and supervised the compilation of the index. Wright has served as liaison with Price. The cutoff date for these listings is 1 June 1984. The compilers welcome addenda and corrigenda.

J.L.W.W. III

Abbreviations

LHL	*A Long and Happy Life*
NFH	*The Names and Faces of Heroes*
GM	*A Generous Man*
L&W	*Love and Work*
PE	*Permanent Errors*
TT	*Things Themselves*
SOE	*The Surface of Earth*
ED	*Early Dark*
PG	*A Palpable God*
SL	*The Source of Light*
VP	*Vital Provisions*
M	*Mustian*
PC	*Private Contentment*

A

Books, Pamphlets, and Broadsides

First Edition: REYNOLDS | PRICE | [swelled rule] | A LONG | AND HAPPY | LIFE | N E W Y O R K | ATHENEUM | 1962

Copyright Page: 'A *portion of this novel appeared in* Encounter | *Copyright* © 1960 *by* Encounter, Ltd. | *Copyright* © 1961 *by Reynolds Price* | *All rights reserved* | *Library of Congress catalog card number* 61–12790 | *Published simultaneously in Canada by* | *Longmans, Green & Company* | *Manufactured in the United States of America by* | *Kingsport Press, Inc., Kingsport, Tennessee* | *Designed by Harry Ford* | *First Edition*'.

Dedication Page: ' F O R | MICHAEL JORDAN | *ch'io ho veduto tutto il verno prima* | *il prun mostrarsi rigido e feroce,* | *poscia portar la rosa in su la cima . . .* | D A N T E, *Paradiso,* XIII'.

Collation: 203 × 127 mm: [1–4¹⁶ 5⁸ 6–7¹⁶]; [i–viii], [1–3] 4–70 [71] 72–148 [149] 150–195 [196–200].

Contents: [i–ii], blank; [iii], half title; [iv], blank; [v], title page; [vi], copyright page; [vii], dedication page; [viii], blank; [1], half title; [2], blank; [3]–195, text; [196], blank; [197], biographical note headed 'REYNOLDS PRICE'; [198–200], blank.

Typography: 33 (pp. 36, 130, 163) or 34 (pp. 73, 146, 179) lines; pages with 33 lines measure 151 (159) × 83 mm, pages with 34 lines measure 156 (163) × 83 mm; 10 lines = 45 mm; face 2.5 (1.5x) mm.

Paper: wove unwatermarked; thickness 0.14 mm (pp. 39–40); total bulk 14.5 mm; yellowish white; uncoated smooth.

Casing: *material*: calico, light brown. *Stamping*: gold. *Front*: 'REYNOLDS PRICE'. *Spine*: '[vert.] REYNOLDS PRICE | [horiz.] [swelled rule] | [vert.] A LONG AND HAPPY LIFE ATHENEUM'. *Back*: unstamped. *Edges*: all edges cut; top edge stained pinkish red. *Endpapers*: wove unwatermarked; thickness 0.18 mm; dark orange; uncoated smooth.

Jacket: three states, priority as follows: *State* 1: total measurement 208 × 501 mm; wove unwatermarked paper; thickness 0.18 mm; both sides uncoated rough; inner side is white; top 133 mm of front and spine and all of back and flaps are white; bright green panel printed on bottom 75 mm of front and spine; lettering and decorations are in yellowish green, bluish green, brownish green, and brown. *Front*: '[bluish green] [three-leaf decoration] [yellowish green] A | [bluish green] Long [three-leaf decoration] | [yellowish green] and | [brownish green] Happy | [bluish green] [three-leaf decoration] Life [yellowish green] by | Reynolds | [brownish green] Price | [to the right of this lettering] [brownish green] [10 lines roman, blurb] | —*Eudora Welty* | [beneath all lettering] [brown] [representation of tree trunk]'. *Spine:* '[vert.] [yellowish green] A [bluish green] Long [yellowish green] and [brownish green] Happy [bluish green] Life | [horiz.] [brown] Atheneum | [vert.] [reversed out in white] by Reynolds Price'. *Back:* '[brown] [16 lines roman, blurb] [yellowish green] —*Stephen Spender* | [brown] [6 lines roman, blurb] [yellowish green] —*Lord David Cecil* | [brown] [14 lines principally roman, blurb] [yellowish green] —*Frances Gray Patton'. Front flap:* '[yellowish green] $3.95 | [brown] [30 lines principally roman, description of book] | [4 lines roman, blurb] | [yellowish green] —*Harper Lee* | [brown] AUTHOR OF *To Kill a Mockingbird'. Back flap:* '[brown] [half-tone of Price] | [yellowish green] *photograph by Wallace Kaufman* | [brown] [13 lines principally roman, biographical note] | [yellowish green] *Jacket design: Janet Halverson'*. *State 2:* identical to State 1 except that the names of Stephen Spender, Lord David Cecil, Frances Gray Patton, Harper Lee, the dashes that precede these names, and the line '*Jacket design: Janet Halverson*' are printed in bluish green rather than yellowish green. *State 3:* identical to State 2 except that the paper is smooth, and the price '$3.95' is missing; probably the BOMC jacket. These three states were first noted by George Bixby in "Blurbs: Welty on Reynolds Price," *Eudora Welty Newsletter,* 1 (Summer 1977).

Notes: published 19 March 1962. $3.95. First printing of 6,000 copies, of which 500 were advance copies in wrappers.

The 500 advance copies of sewn signatures in wrappers are identical to the first trade impression except for the wrappers: thickness 0.20 mm; both sides uncoated smooth; yellow; all lettering in black. *Front:* 'This is an advance copy of | A LONG | AND HAPPY LIFE | A NOVEL BY | REYNOLDS PRICE | [swelled rule] | *Eudora Welty* | [4 lines roman, blurb] | *Stephen Spender* | [14 lines roman, blurb] | *Lord David Cecil* | [5 lines roman, blurb] | *To be published by* ATHENEUM *January 5, 1962 $3.95'. Spine:* '[vert.] REYNOLDS PRICE: *A LONG AND HAPPY LIFE* ATHENEUM'. *Back:* blank. *Edges:* all edges cut and unstained.

Sets of page proofs in light blue paper covers, bound with a dark blue plastic ring binder, were also issued by the publisher. A white paper label printed in black and red is pasted on the front cover. The publication date given on these copies is 13 Sept. 1961 and the price $3.50. (George Bixby to West, 7 May 1979.)

Atheneum has published eight trade printings of LHL: first printing, January 1962; second printing, February 1962; third printing, March 1962; fourth printing, April 1962; fifth printing, June 1962; sixth printing, October 1964; seventh printing, December 1966; eighth printing, November 1968.

The novel was a Book-of-the-Month Club selection in 1962; these copies can be identified by the usual blind-stamped round dot on the back of the casing and by the absence of a price on the front jacket flap. It was also published in its entirety in *Harper's Magazine*, 224 (April 1962), 105–68; offprints of this appearance were issued. LHL appeared in a pirated offset replating in Taiwan, probably published in 1962 or 1963. LHL and GM appeared together in a double paperback for Quality Paperback Book Club in 1976; this volume is an offset replating of the second trade impressions of both books, with pagination unaltered.

Editions subsequent to the first are:

A1b   London: Chatto and Windus, 1962. 212 pp. 16s. net. Cased in imitation cloth, with jacket. 4,900 copies. Published 22 March 1962. The only true British edition (i.e., fresh typesetting) of one of Price's books.

A1c   New York: Avon Book Division, [1963]. 160 pp. Avon S–119. 60¢. Wrappers. Published March 1963.

A1d   Harmondsworth: Penguin, 1964. 176 pp. Penguin 2105. 3/6. Wrappers. 20,000 copies. Published 30 April 1964.

A1e   New York: Avon Library, 1965. 176 pp. Avon Library SS8. 60¢. Wrappers. Published June 1965.

A1f   New York: Avon Library, 1969. 224 pp. Avon Library NS43. 95¢. Wrappers. Published July 1969.

An excerpt from LHL has appeared in *Contemporary American Novelists*, ed. Jean Rouberol and Henri Kerst (Paris: Masson et Cie, 1973), pp. 100–102 (the passage from 169.1–171.26 in the first edition).

A2a   *The Names and Faces of Heroes*   1963

First Edition: REYNOLDS | PRICE | [swelled rule] | THE NAMES | AND FACES OF | HEROES | N E W   Y O R K | ATHENEUM | 1963

Copyright Page: 'These stories have appeared, some in different forms, in | THE ARCHIVE, COUNTRY BEAUTIFUL, DUKE UNIVERSITY | ALUMNI REGISTER, SHENANDOAH, THE VIRGINIA QUARTERLY | REVIEW *and an anthology*, WINTER'S TALES | *Copyright 1954*, © *1961*, © *1962*, © *1963 by Reynolds Price* | *Copyright* © *1958 by Macmillan & Company, Ltd.* | *All rights reserved* | *Library of Congress catalog card number 63–12414* | *Published simultaneously in Canada by* | *McClelland & Stewart Ltd.* | *Manufactured in the United States of America by* | *Kingsport Press, Inc., Kingsport, Tennessee* | *Designed by Harry Ford* | *First Edition*'.

Dedication Page: 'IN MEMORY OF | WILL PRICE | FOR | ELIZABETH PRICE | F O R | WILL, MY BROTHER'.

Collation: 202 × 126 mm: [1–6¹⁶]; [i–xii], [1–3] 4–43 [44] 45–53 [54] 55–63 [64] 65–92 [93] 94–109 [110] 111–137 [138] 139–178 [179–180].

Contents: [i], blank; [ii], list of books by Price; [iii], half title; [iv], blank; [v], title page; [vi], copyright page; [vii], dedication page; [viii], blank; [ix], table of contents; [x], blank; [xi], epigraph from William Blake; [xii], blank; [1], half title; [2], blank; [3]–178, text; [179], blank; [180], biographical note headed 'REYNOLDS PRICE'. This collection of short stories contains "A Chain of Love," "The Warrior Princess Ozimba," "Michael Egerton," "The Anniversary," "Troubled Sleep," "Uncle Grant," and "The Names and Faces of Heroes."

Running Titles: head: '[titles of individual stories in italics] | [titles of individual stories in italics]'.

Typography: 30 lines (p. 77); 152 (157) × 84 mm; 10 lines = 50 mm; face 2.5 (1.5x) mm.

Paper: wove unwatermarked; thickness 0.14 mm (pp. 137–38); total bulk 13.5 mm; yellowish white; uncoated smooth.

Casing: material: calico, blue. Stamping: gold. Front: 'REYNOLDS PRICE'. Spine: '[vert.] REYNOLDS PRICE | [horiz.] [swelled rule] | [vert.] THE NAMES & FACES OF HEROES ATHENEUM'. Back: unstamped. Edges: all edges cut; top edge stained blue. Endpapers: wove unwatermarked; thickness 0.18 mm; brownish red; uncoated smooth.

Jacket: total measurement 209 × 498 mm; wove unwatermarked paper; thickness 0.19 mm; both sides uncoated smooth; inner side is white; back and flaps are white; front and spine are blue; lettering and decorations are in blue, orange, yellow, brown, yellowish green, and brownish green. Front: '[reversed out in white] Reynolds Price | [within a wreath of orange, yellow, brown, yellowish green, and brownish green leaves] [yellowish green] The | [orange] Names | [brownish green] and [yellowish green] Faces | [brown] of | [yellow] Heroes | [white] Stories | by | [bow of the wreath] | the | author | of | "A Long | and Happy | Life" '. Spine: '[vert.] [yellow] The Names and Faces of Heroes | [white] Reynolds Price | [at the base of the spine is an orange leaf; reversed out in white within the leaf, reading diagonally upper left to lower right, is 'Atheneum']'. Back: '[orange] About A Long and Happy Life | a novel by Reynolds Price | [blue] [7 lines principally roman, quote from review] | Honor Tracy, The New Leader | [8 lines roman, quote from review] | William Barrett, The Atlantic | [3 lines roman, quote from review] Dorothy Parker, Esquire | [6 lines principally roman, quote from review] The Times Literary Supplement | [4 lines principally roman, quote from review] Charles Poore, The New York Times | [3 lines roman, quote from review] Granville Hicks, Saturday Review'. Front flap: '[orange] $3.95 | [blue] [29 lines principally roman, description of book] | [orange] Jacket design: Janet Halverson'. Back flap: '[blue] [halftone of

Price] | [orange] *Photograph: Alfredo De Luise* | [14 lines principally roman, biographical note]'.

Notes: published 25 June 1963. $3.95. First printing of 6,000 copies.

Atheneum has published three trade printings of NFH: first printing, May 1963; second printing, August 1963; third printing, November 1966.

Atheneum also published a paperback offset replating of NFH on 17 Sept. 1973.

The Bixby collection includes a set of unbound long galleys for NFH; the label pasted on the first galley gives a projected publication date of 15 June 1963. Not examined by the compiler.

The sheets of the British "edition," published 29 Sept. 1963 in London by Chatto and Windus, were printed in the United States from the Atheneum plates. The title page and copyright page in the first gathering were altered for British publication before the sheets were printed. These flat sheets were shipped to England, where the casing (blue imitation cloth, white wove endpapers) was added. The Chatto and Windus jacket was also printed, with slight alterations, in this country. This British "edition" consisted of 2,750 copies; retail price was 18s. There has been only one true edition subsequent to the first:

A2b New York: Avon Books, 1966. 144 pp. Avon S225. 60¢. Wrappers.

A3a   *A Generous Man*   1966

First Edition: REYNOLDS | PRICE | [swelled rule] | A GENEROUS | MAN | N E W   Y O R K | ATHENEUM | 1966

Copyright page: '*Copyright* © *1966 by Reynolds Price* | *All rights reserved* | *Library of Congress catalog card number 66–16357* | *Published simultaneously in Canada by* | *McClelland & Stewart Ltd.* | *Manufactured in the United States of America by* | *Kingsport Press, Inc., Kingsport, Tennessee* | *Designed by Harry Ford* | *First Edition*'.

Dedication Page: '*F O R* | RAPHAEL JONES | *Come degnasti d'accedere al monte?* | *non sapei tu che qui è l'uom felice?* | D A N T E , *Purgatorio*, XXX'.

Collation: 203 × 127 mm: [1–9¹⁶]; [i–viii], [1–3] 4–79 [80] 81–244 [245] 246–275 [276–280].

Contents: [i], blank; [ii], list of books by Price; [iii], half title; [iv], blank; [v], title page; [vi], copyright page; [vii], dedication page; [viii], blank; [1], half title; [2], blank; [3]–275, text; [276], blank; [277], biographical note headed 'REYNOLDS PRICE'; [278–280], blank.

Typography: 32 (pp. 69, 132, 207) or 33 (pp. 24, 173, 238) lines; pages with 32 lines measure 152 (160) × 83 mm, pages with 33 lines measure 157 (164) × 83 mm; 10 lines = 47 mm; face 2.5 (1.5x) mm.

Paper: wove unwatermarked; thickness 0.14 mm (pp. 171–72); total bulk 20 mm; yellowish white; uncoated smooth.

Casing: *material*: calico, dark green. *Stamping*: gold. *Front*: 'REYN-OLDS PRICE'. *Spine*: '[vert.] REYNOLDS PRICE | [horiz.] [swelled rule] | [vert.] A GENEROUS MAN ATHENEUM'. *Back*: unstamped. *Edges*: all edges cut; top edge stained pinkish red. *Endpapers*: wove unwatermarked; thickness 0.19 mm; yellowish green; uncoated smooth.

Jacket: total measurement 208 × 513 mm; wove unwatermarked paper; thickness 0.14 mm; inner side uncoated smooth, outer side coated glossy; both sides are white; lettering and decorations on outer side are in green, yellowish green, red, gray, brown, and black. *Front*: '[against a representation of an apple tree with a snake coiled around its trunk and through its branches—the leaves in green, the apples in red, the trunk in gray, and the snake in brown and black] [yellowish green] A Generous | Man | Reynolds Price | [to the right of 'Man'] [black] a novel by the author of | "A Long and Happy Life" '. *Spine*: '[the leaves of the tree and one apple are carried over from the front to the spine] [vert.] [yellowish green] Reynolds Price [green] A Generous Man | [horiz.] [black] Atheneum'. *Back*: '[black-and-white photo of Price, bled off top and sides] | [green] Reynolds Price | [black] [17 lines roman, autobiographical note by Price] | [red] *(continued on back flap)*'. *Front flap*: '[yellowish green] $4.95 | [black] [38 lines principally roman, description of book] | [red] *Jacket design: Janet Halverson*'. *Back flap*: '[red] *(continued from back of jacket)* | [black] [33 lines principally roman, remainder of autobiographical note] | [green] *Photograph by Joel Arrington*'.

Notes: published 25 March 1966. $4.95. First printing of 10,000 copies, of which 500 were advance copies in wrappers.

Sets of the page proofs of GM were issued in advance of formal publication. Each set consists of 288 leaves printed on the rectos only. The title page is identical to that of the first trade printing; the third line of the copyright page reads '*Library of Congress catalog card number 00–000*'. Page [i] is headed '1FM—38921 Generous Man'. Several pages bear the legend 'Above Page is —— lines SHORT' at the bottom; there are 285 numbered leaves in this advance issue but, as a result of repaging, only 275 numbered pages in the published book. Each set of page proofs is perforated along the left-hand margin and held together by a blue plastic ring-binding device. Covers on all sets observed are of unprinted light blue wove paper 0.21 mm thick. Five hundred advance copies consisting of sewn signatures in wrappers were also issued; trade endpapers were attached, and the trade jacket was glued on at the spine to function as the wrapper.

Atheneum has published three trade printings of GM: first printing, February 1966; second printing, March 1966; third printing, April 1966. The novel was a Literary Guild selection in Spring 1966. The British "edition," published 12 January 1967 by Chatto and Windus, is an offset replating of the Atheneum text, printed in London by Lowe & Brydone. There were 4,000 copies printed; retail price was 21s. GM appeared with LHL in a double paperback in 1976; see A1, *Notes*. There have been two editions subsequent to the first:

A3b   New York: Signet, 1967. 192 pp. Signet T3072. 75¢. Wrappers. Anne S. Carter of NAL to West, 19 July 1979, states that there are "currently over 130,000 copies [of this edition] in print." Published 1 April 1967.

A3c   New York: Avon, 1973. 224 pp. Bard Books, 15123. $1.65. Wrappers. Published August 1973.

A4   *The Thing Itself* (Pamphlet)   1966

First Edition: [Self-wrappers] The Thing Itself | by | Reynolds Price

Copyright Page: 'This is the substance of an address by | Reynolds Price to the Annual Dinner | of the Friends of Duke University | Library, April 28, 1966. | Copyright ©, 1966 by the New York Times Company. | Reprinted by permission.' The verso of the front self-wrapper is the copyright page.

Collation: 228 × 152 mm: [1⁴]; [1–8].

Contents: [1], title page; [2], copyright page; [3–7], text; [8], blank.

Typography: 44 lines (p. [6]); 189 × 114 mm; 10 lines = 42 mm; face 2.67 (2.0x) mm.

Paper: wove; watermarked '*Ticonderoga* | *Text*'; thickness 0.17 mm (pp. [1–2]); total bulk 0.68 mm; yellowish white; uncoated smooth.

Note: The publication records at Duke University Library for *The Thing Itself* no longer survive, but correspondence with Price in the library's files indicates that publication was in June 1966 and that the press run was probably 750 copies. Not for sale.

A5   *Love and Work*   1968

First Edition: REYNOLDS | PRICE | [swelled rule] | LOVE AND | WORK | NEW YORK | ATHENEUM | 1968

Copyright Page: 'Copyright © 1967, 1968 by Reynolds Price | All rights reserved | Library of Congress catalog card number 68–22422 | Published simultaneously in Canada by | McClelland & Stewart Ltd. | Manufactured in the United States of America by | Kingsport Press, Inc., Kingsport, Tennessee | Designed by Harry Ford | First Edition'.

Dedication Page: 'FOR | WILLIAM PRICE | AND | PIA | AND | MARIE ELIZABETH'.

Collation: 204 × 126 mm: [1–5^{16}]; [i–xii], [1–3] 4–44 [45] 46–80 [81] 82–113 [114] 115–143 [144–148].

Contents: [i–iii], blank; [iv], list of books by Price; [v], half title; [vi], blank; [vii], title page; [viii], copyright page; [ix], dedication page; [x], blank; [xi], epigraph from Hofmannsthal; [xii], blank; [1], half title; [2], blank; [3]–143, text; [144], blank; [145], biographical note headed 'REYNOLDS PRICE'; [146–148], blank.

Typography: 32 lines (p. 108); 152 (158) × 84 mm; 10 lines = 47 mm; face 2.5 (1.5x) mm.

Paper: wove unwatermarked; thickness 0.17 mm (pp. 85–86); total bulk 13.5 mm; yellowish white; uncoated smooth.

Casing: *material*: calico, dark blue. *Stamping*: gold. *Front*: 'REYNOLDS PRICE'. *Spine*: '[vert.] REYNOLDS PRICE | [horiz.] [swelled rule] | [vert.] LOVE AND WORK ATHENEUM'. *Back*: unstamped. *Edges*: all edges cut; top edge stained brownish yellow. *Endpapers*: wove unwatermarked; thickness 0.18 mm; greenish gray; uncoated smooth.

Jacket: total measurement 209 × 498 mm; wove unwatermarked paper; thickness 0.16 mm; inner side uncoated smooth, outer side coated glossy; inner side is white; back and flaps are white; front is blue; spine is black; lettering and decorations are in light green, white, blue, and black. *Front*: '[light green] LOVE | [reversed out in white] & | [light green] WORK | [white] Reynolds Price | A NOVEL | [black] silhouettes of two leafless trees and one leafless seedling]'. *Spine*: '[vert.] [light green] LOVE [white] & [light green] WORK [white] Reynolds Price [blue] ATHENEUM'. *Back*: '[black] About [blue] A Generous Man | [black] a novel by Reynolds Price | [3 lines roman, blurb] [blue] *Allen Tate* | [black] [4 lines principally roman, quote from review] | [blue] *Conrad Knickerbocker, The New York Times* | [black] [12 lines principally roman, quote from review] [blue] *William McPherson, Life* | [black] [8 lines roman, quote from review] [blue] *Newsweek* | [black] [4 lines principally roman, quote from review] [blue] *Time*'. *Front flap*: '[light green] $4.50 | [black] [27 lines principally roman, description of book] | [blue] *Jacket design: Janet Halverson*'. *Back flap*: '[black-and-white photo of Price, bled off top] | [blue] *Photograph by Wallace Kaufman* | [black] [17 lines principally roman, biographical note]'.

Notes: published 29 May 1968. $4.50. First printing of 10,000 copies.

Page proofs were issued in light blue wrappers bound with a dark blue plastic ring binder. A white label printed in black and red is pasted on the front wrapper. Not examined by the compiler.

Atheneum has published only one impression of L&W. The British "edition," published 24 October 1968 by Chatto and Windus, is an offset replating of the Atheneum text, printed in Cardiff by William Lewis Ltd. There were 1,250 copies manufactured; retail price was 25s. On 17 February 1975 Atheneum published an offset replating in paperback, with corrections by Price. There has been no separate edition of L&W subsequent to the first. A condensed English-language edition was one of four titles included in *Four Star Condensations*, vol. 5 (Bombay: Vakils, Feffer and Simons Private Ltd., n.d.).

A6   *Late Warning* (Limited Signed Edition)   1968

First Edition: [purple] L A T E | W A R N I N G | [black] *four poems by* | [purple] *Reynolds* | *Price* | [black] ALBONDOCANI PRESS : NEW YORK : 1968

Copyright Page: '© 1966 by Reynolds Price   © 1968 by Reynolds Price | Acknowledgment is made to Atheneum for "My Parents, | Winter 1926" where it appeared in a different form as part | of *Love and Work*; to *Esquire* where "Life for Life" first | appeared; to *The Southern Review* where "The Knowledge | of My Mother's Coming Death" first appeared. "Design | for a Tomb" appears for the first time here.'

Collation: 203 × 127 mm; [1¹⁴]; [i–ii], [1–7] 8 [9] 10–15 [16] 17–19 [20] 21–22 [23–26].

Contents: [i–ii], blank; [1], half title; [2], black-and-white photo of Price's parents, pasted within a heavy black border 4 mm thick; [3], title page; [4], copyright page; [5], table of contents; [6], blank; [7]–22, text; [23], statement of limitation and colophon; [24], 'Printed by William Ferguson | Cambridge, Massachusetts | Frontispiece photograph reproduced by | The Meriden Gravure Company | Meriden, Connecticut | Albondocani Press Publication No. 4'; [25–26], blank. This collection contains "My Parents, Winter 1926," "The Knowledge of My Mother's Coming Death," "Life for Life," and "Design for a Tomb."

Typography: 30 lines (p. 10); 147 (155) × 89 mm; 10 lines = 49 mm; face 3.0 (2.0x) mm.

Paper: laid; chainlines 26 mm apart; watermarked 'FABRIANO (ITALY)'; thickness 0.15 mm (pp. 11–12); total bulk 2 mm; light brown; uncoated rough.

Sewn Wrappers: wove unwatermarked paper; thickness 0.55 mm; black; uncoated smooth.

Sewn Jacket: total measurement 208 × 456 mm; unwatermarked laid paper, chainlines 26 mm apart; inner side brownish white; outer side marbled in maroon, brown, black, and brownish orange; white paper label measuring 31 × 55 mm pasted on front 51 mm from top and 39 mm from spine, label printed in black: 'LATE WARNING | Reynolds Price'.

> *Notes:* published 26 December 1968. $15.00. 176 numbered copies. Four overrun copies, out of series, also signed by Price.
>
> Page [23] reads: *'This first edition of* | LATE WARNING | *published in December 1968* | *is limited to* | *one hundred and seventy-six copies.* | *The type is Electra,* | *the paper is Italian Fabriano,* | *and the hand-sewn wrappers are* | *a French marble paper.* | *One hundred and fifty copies* | *numbered 1–150 are for sale.* | *Twenty-six copies* | *lettered A–Z for the use* | *of the author and publisher* | *are not for sale.* | *All copies are signed* | *by the author.* | *This is number* | [arabic numerals written in red ballpoint pen] | [Price's signature in black fountain pen]'.

A7   *Torso of an Archaic Apollo* (Christmas Greeting)   1969

First Edition: [Self-wrappers] [vert. bottom to top] TORSO OF AN ARCHAIC APOLLO | BY REYNOLDS PRICE — AFTER RILKE | [horiz.] [drawing of a nude male torso]

Copyright Page: '© 1969 by Reynolds Price'.

Collation: 168 × 117 mm: [1²]; [1–4].

Contents: two states, no priority: *State 1:* 'HOLIDAY GREETINGS | AND | BEST WISHES | FOR THE | COMING YEAR'; [2], copyright page; [3], text of poem; [4], statement of limitation. *State 2:* page [1] reads: 'HOLIDAY . . . YEAR | FROM | ALBONDO-CANI PRESS | AND | AMPERSAND BOOKS'.

Typography: approx. 22 lines (p. [3]); 94 (104) × 87 mm; 10 lines = 47 mm; face 2.67 (1.67x) mm.

Paper: wove unwatermarked; thickness 0.20 mm (pp. [1–2]); total bulk 0.40 mm; yellowish white; uncoated rough.

Stapled Self-Wrappers: wove unwatermarked; thickness o.30 mm; light brown; uncoated rough. The fore edge of the front of the self-wrapper is an uncut or "deckle" edge. Issued in a white envelope with heavy gray cardboard stiffener.

Notes: published 12 December 1969. Not for sale. 320 copies printed, 210 of State 1 and 110 of State 2.

Page [4] reads: *'This first printing of* | TORSO OF AN ARCHAIC APOLLO | *published in December 1969* | *is limited to* | *three hundred copies* | *to be used* | *as a holiday greeting* | *by the author and publisher.* | *None are for sale.* | Cover drawing by Robert Dunn | *Printed by* | *William Ferguson* | *for* | *Albondocani Press'.*

A8 **Permanent Errors** 1970

First Edition: REYNOLDS | PRICE | [swelled rule] | PERMANENT | ERRORS | N E W Y O R K | ATHENEUM | 1970

Copyright Page: *'Some of these pieces have appeared—in earlier* | *forms—in* Esquire, Playboy, Red Clay Reader, | Shenandoah, The Southern Review, Vogue; *and* | *the group* LATE WARNINGS *was published in 1969* | *in a limited edition by the Albondocani Press.* | *Copyright* © *1963, 1964, 1965, 1966, 1967, 1968,* | *1969, 1970 by Reynolds Price* | *All rights reserved* | *Library of Congress catalog card number 70–124974* | *Published simultaneously in Canada by* | *McClelland and Stewart Ltd* | *Manufactured in the United States of America by* | *Kingsport Press, Inc., Kingsport, Tennessee* | *Designed by Harry Ford* | *First Edition'.*

Dedication Page: 'F O R | EUDORA WELTY'.

Collation: 203 × 126 mm: [1–7¹⁶ 8⁸ 9¹⁶]; [2], [i–vii] viii [ix–xii], [1–3] 4–11 [12] 13–16 [17] 18–50 [51] 52–87 [88–91] 92 [93] 94–98 [99] 100–101 [102] 103 [104] 105–107 [108] 109–111 [112–115] 116–134 [135] 136–140 [141] 142–143 [144–145] 146 [147] 148–150 [151] 152–154 [155–157] 158–253 [254–258].

Contents: [1], blank; [2], list of books by Price; [i], half title; [ii], blank; [iii], title page; [iv], copyright page; [v], dedication page; [vi], blank; [vii]–viii, introductory note headed 'TO THE READER' on [vii]; [ix], table of contents; [x], blank; [xi], epigraph poem by Price after Rilke; [xii], blank; [1]–253, text; [254], blank; [255], biographical note headed 'REYNOLDS PRICE'; [256–258], blank. This collection is divided into four sections: Section One ('FOOL'S EDUCATION') contains "The Happiness of Others," "A Dog's Death," "Scars," and "Waiting at Dachau"; Section Two ('ELEGIES') contains "Late Warnings," "Invitation, for Jessie Rehder," and "Summer Games"; Section Three

('HOME LIFE') contains "Truth and Lies" and "Good and Bad Dreams"; Section Four ('THE ALCHEMIST') contains "Walking Lessons."

Running Titles: *head*: '[titles of sections in italics] | [titles of individual items in italics]'.

Typography: 33 lines (p. 58); 152 (158) × 84 mm; 10 lines = 45 mm; face 2.5 (1.5x) mm.

Paper: wove unwatermarked; thickness 0.16 mm (pp. 129–30); total bulk 22 mm; yellowish white; uncoated smooth.

Casing: *material*: calico, brown. *Stamping*: gold. *Front*: 'REYNOLDS PRICE'. *Spine*: '[vert.] REYNOLDS PRICE | [horiz.] [swelled rule] | [vert.] PERMANENT ERRORS ATHENEUM'. *Back*: unstamped. *Edges*: all edges cut; top edge stained orange. *Endpapers*: wove unwatermarked; thickness 0.18 mm; red; uncoated smooth.

Jacket: total measurement 208 × 505 mm; wove unwatermarked paper; thickness 0.15 mm; inner side uncoated smooth; outer side coated glossy; inner side is white; front, back, and flaps are white; spine is black; lettering and decorations are in pinkish red, red, orange, yellowish orange, yellow, and black. *Front*: '[black] Permanent Errors | [orange] Stories by | [black] Reynolds Price | [photo of Price's parents within a black-and-white yin-yang circle; behind the photo are concentric circles in red, orange, yellowish orange, and yellow]'. *Spine* '[vert.] [all lettering reversed out in white] Reynolds Price | [horiz.] Atheneum | [vert.] Permanent Errors'. *Back*: '[pinkish red] About [black] Love and Work | [pinkish red] a novel by Reynolds Price | [black] [10 lines roman, quote from review] | [pinkish red] **Peter Wolfe**, Book World | [black] [7 lines roman, quote from review] | [pinkish red] **Vernon Scannell**, The New Statesman | [black] [5 lines roman, quote from review] | [pinkish red] **Louis D. Rubin, Jr.**, The Washington Star | [black] [9 lines roman, quote from review] | [pinkish red] **Francis King**, The London Sunday Telegraph'. *Front flap*: '[pinkish red] $6.50 | [black] [41 lines principally roman, description of book]'. *Back flap*: '[black-and-white photo of Price, bled off top] | [pinkish red] Photograph: John Menapace | [black] Reynolds Price | [21 lines principally roman, biographical note] | [pinkish red] Jacket design: Janet Halverson'.

Notes: published 23 September 1970. $6.50. First printing of 5,000 copies.
    Atheneum has published only one clothbound printing of PE. The British "edition" (Chatto and Windus, 25 March 1971) consists of sheets printed in the U.S. as an overrun from the Atheneum first printing. The title page and copyright page in the first gathering were altered for British publication before the extra sheets were printed. The sheets were folded and sewn in this country, and the endpapers (identical to those of the Atheneum first

printing) were affixed here. The unbound books were then shipped to England, where the Chatto casing (red imitation' cloth) and jacket (0.8 mm thickness) were added. There were 1,500 copies of this British "edition" prepared; retail price was 175p. There has been no edition of PE subsequent to the first, but Atheneum has published an offset replating in paperback (1980), with authorial corrections.

A9   *Two Theophanies* (Christmas Greeting)   1971

First Edition: [Self-wrappers] [silver] [the following words are a reproduction of Price's handwriting] Two Theophanies | [Hebrew letters surrounded by lines that give an aureole effect] | [reproduction of Price's handwriting] Genesis 32 + John 21

Copyright Page: none; the copyright notice is on p. [4].

Collation: 168 × 120 mm: [1²]; [1–4].

Contents: [1], '[first letter a display cap] Every good hope for Christmas 1971 | and for all of 1972'; [2–3], text of theophanies; [4], statement of limitation and copyright notice.

Typography: 28 lines (p. [3]); 129 × 90 mm; 10 lines = 47 mm; face 2.5 (2.0x) mm. All text printing is in brown ink.

Paper: wove unwatermarked; thickness 0.18 mm (pp. [3–4]); total bulk 0.36 mm; brown; uncoated smooth.

Stapled Self-Wrappers: two states, priority as follows: *State* 1: wove unwatermarked paper; thickness 0.34 mm; purple; uncoated smooth. *Front*: title page. *Back*: alpha-omega symbol in silver. *State* 2: identical to State 1 except that the wrapper paper is light gray and all printing on it is in black ink. According to Price, "only a few" copies of State 2 were prepared. Issued in an envelope.

Notes: published 12 December 1971. Not for sale. 215 copies.
    Page [4] reads: 'This first printing of | TWO THEOPHANIES | *in versions by Reynolds Price* | is limited to | two hundred copies | for his friends, | at Christmas 1971. | Printed by | David Southern | © 1971 by Reynolds Price'.

A10   *Things Themselves*   1972

First Edition: REYNOLDS PRICE | [swelled rule] | THINGS | THEMSELVES | ESSAYS & SCENES | N E W   Y O R K | ATHE-NEUM | 1972

Copyright Page: '*Copyright* © 1968, 1969, 1970, 1971, 1972 *by* | *Reynolds Price* | FIVE SKETCHES FOR A SCREENPLAY *copyright* © | 1972 *by Atheneum Publishers Inc.* | A REASONABLE GUIDE THROUGH PERILOUS SEAS | *copyright* © 1964 *by The Washington Post* | FRIGHTENING GIFT *copyright* © 1970 *by The* | *Washington Post* | THE WINGS OF THE DOVE: A SINGLE COMBAT | *copyright* © 1970 *by Charles E. Merrill* | *Publishing Company* | DODO, PHOENIX OR TOUGH OLD COCK? *copyright* © | 1972 *by L.Q.C. Lamar Society* | FOUR ABRAHAMS, FOUR ISAACS BY REMBRANDT | *copyright* © 1972 *by Prose Publishers* | *Incorporated* | *All rights reserved* | *Library of Congress catalog card number* 79–190398 | *Published simultaneously in Canada by* | *McClelland & Stewart Ltd* | *Manufactured in the United States of America by* | *Kingsport Press, Inc., Kingsport, Tennessee* | *Designed by Harry Ford* | *First Edition*'.

Dedication Page: 'F O R | PHYLLIS ABBOTT PEACOCK'.

Collation: 203 × 127 mm; [1–9^{16}]; [2], [i–vii] viii–xv [xvi], [1–3] 4–22 [23] 24–69 [70] 71–90 [91] 92–108 [109] 110–113 [114] 115–138 [139] 140–142 [143] 144–163 [164] 165–175 [176] 177–213 [214] 215–259 [260] 261–262 [4] 263–269 [270]. The four unnumbered pages following p. 262 are a tipped-in two-leaf gathering which prints reproductions of three etchings and an oil painting by Rembrandt.

Contents: [1], blank; [2], list of books by Price; [i], half title; [ii], blank; [iii], title page; [iv], copyright page; [v], dedication page; [vi], blank; [vii]–xv, introduction headed 'TO THE READER' on [vii]; [xvi], table of contents; [1], half title; [2], blank; [3]–269, text; [270], biographical note headed 'REYNOLDS PRICE'. This collection contains "Dodging Apples," "Five Sketches for a Screenplay," "News for the Mineshaft," "*Pylon*—The Posture of Worship," "A Reasonable Guide through Perilous Seas," "The Onlooker, Smiling," "Frightening Gift," "*The Wings of the Dove*—A Single Combat," "Dodo, Phoenix, or Tough Old Cock?", "For Ernest Hemingway," "Poem Doctrinal and Exemplary to a Nation," and "Four Abrahams, Four Isaacs by Rembrandt."

Running Titles: *head*: '*Things Themselves* | [titles of individual essays in italics]'.

Typography: 35 lines (p. 154); 155 (161) × 84 mm; 10 lines = 44 mm; face 2.5 (1.5x) mm.

Paper: wove unwatermarked; thickness 0.16 mm (pp. 213–214); total bulk 23 mm; yellowish white; uncoated smooth.

Casing: *material*: linen, brownish white with brown flecks. *Stamping*: gold. *Front*: 'REYNOLDS PRICE'. *Spine*: '[vert.] REYNOLDS

PRICE | [horiz.] [swelled rule] | [vert.] THINGS THEMSELVES ATH-
ENEUM'. *Back*: unstamped. *Edges*: all edges cut; top edge stained
brown. *Endpapers*: wove unwatermarked; thickness o.19 mm; slate
gray; uncoated smooth.

Jacket: total measurement 208 × 506 mm; wove unwatermarked paper; thickness o.13 mm; inner side uncoated smooth; outer side coated
glossy; inner side is white; back and flaps are white; front and spine are
printed in brown and black background panels; lettering is brown,
black, and reversed out in white. *Front*: '[reversed out in white] [against
a brown panel] REYNOLDS | PRICE | [heavy white rule] | [against a
black panel] THINGS | THEMSELVES | [heavy white rule] | [against
a brown panel] ESSAYS & SCENES | BY THE AUTHOR OF | A
Long and Happy Life | *A Generous Man* | *Love and Work*'. *Spine*: '[vert.
in two lines] [reversed out in white] [against a brown panel] THINGS |
THEMSELVES | [horiz.] [heavy white rule] | [vert. in two lines]
[against a black panel] REYNOLDS | PRICE | [horiz.] [heavy white
rule] | [vert.] [black] [against a brown panel] ATHENEUM'. *Back*:
'[brown] REYNOLDS PRICE | [black] [2 lines roman, quote from re-
view] | [brown] *Theodore Solotaroff*, [black] *The Saturday Review* (1970)
| [4 lines roman, blurb for LHL] [brown] *Eudora Welty* | [8 lines roman,
quote from a review of NFH] | [brown] *Richard Gilman*, [black] *The New
York Times Book Review* | [4 lines roman, quote from a review of GM] |
[brown] *Conrad Knickerbocker*, [black] *The New York Times* | [9 lines
roman, quote from a review of L&W] | [brown] *Francis King*, [black]
The Sunday Telegraph (London) | [4 lines roman, quote from a review
of PE] [brown] *Guy Davenport*, [black] *The New York Times Book Review*'. Each blurb or quote begins with the title of the Price book in
boldface full caps, printed in brown. *Front flap*: '[brown] *Illustrated*
$8.95 | [black] [10 lines roman, description of the book by Price] |
[brown] [8 lines roman, publisher's blurb] | [black] [15 lines principally
roman, publisher's blurb]'. *Back flap*: '[black-and-white photo of Price,
bled off top] | [brown] *Photograph*: *John Menapace* | [black] REYN-
OLDS PRICE | [brown] [22 lines principally roman, biographical
note]'.

Notes: published 22 May 1972. $8.95. First printing of 3,500 copies.
Atheneum has published only one impression of TT. There has been no
British publication, nor has there been an edition of TT subsequent to the
first.

A11 *The Fourth Eclogue of Vergil* (Christmas Greeting) 1972

First Edition: [Reproduction of Dürer engraving] | [the following words
are a reproduction of Price's handwriting] The | Fourth Eclogue of Ver-
gil | translated for Christmas | 1972

Copyright Page: none; at the bottom of p. [2] this copyright notice is printed: '© Reynolds Price 1972'.

Collation: 178 × 125 mm: [1²]; [1–4]. A single sheet folded once on a vertical axis.

Contents: [1], title page; [2–3], text; [4], reproduction of an engraving by Cranach and colophon.

Typography: 31 lines (p. [3]); 141 × 70 mm; 10 lines = 45 mm; face 2.33 (1.5x) mm. All printing is in brownish red ink.

Paper: wove unwatermarked; thickness 0.34 mm (pp. [3–4]); total bulk 0.68 mm; light brown; uncoated smooth. The fore edge of the first leaf is an uncut or "deckle" edge, stained brown.

Notes: published 15 December 1972. Not for sale. 225 copies.
Page [4] reads: 'This first printing of the Fourth Eclogue of Vergil | in a translation by Reynolds Price | is for his friends, at Christmas 1972. | The Virgin and Child revealed to St. John is by Dürer, | the Christ Child by Cranach. | Printed by David Southern.'

A12   *An Apocryphal Hymn of Jesus* (Christmas Greeting) 1973

First Edition: [Reproduction of Blake drawing] | [the following words are a reproduction of Price's handwriting] An | Apocryphal | Hymn of Jesus | translated for Christmas 1973

Copyright Page: none; the copyright notice is at the foot of p. [2].

Collation: 178 × 127 mm: [1²]; [1–4]. A single sheet folded once on a vertical axis.

Contents: [1], title page; [2–3], text; [4], drawing by Blake and colophon.

Typography: 28 lines (p. [2]); 125 × 84 mm; 10 lines = 42 mm; face 2.5 (1.67x) mm. All printing is in purple ink.

Paper: wove unwatermarked; thickness 0.38 mm (pp. [3–4]); total bulk 0.76 mm; outer side grayish white, inner side white; uncoated smooth.

Notes: published 15 December 1973. Not for sale. 215 copies.
Page [4] reads: 'This first printing of a Hymn of Jesus | from the Apocryphal Acts of John | in a translation by Reynolds Price | is for his friends, at Christmas 1973. | The figures dancing are by William Blake. | Printed by David Southern.'

A13 *Presence and Absence* 1973 [1974]
(Limited Signed Edition)

First Edition: [Double title page] [left-hand page] BRUCCOLI CLARK | BLOOMFIELD HILLS, MICHIGAN | AND | COLUMBIA, SOUTH CAROLINA | 1973 | [right-hand page] PRESENCE | AND | ABSENCE | [ornament] | Versions | from the Bible | by | Reynolds Price

Copyright Page: '[logo] A Bruccoli-Clark Collector's Edition | COPYRIGHT © 1970, 1974 BY REYNOLDS PRICE | ALL RIGHTS RESERVED | PRINTED IN THE UNITED STATES OF AMERICA'.

Collation: 222 × 143 mm: [1–3^8]; [1–8] 9–44 [45–48].

Contents: [1], statement of limitation; [2–3], double title page; [4], copyright page; [5], table of contents; [6], blank; [7], half title; [8], blank; 9–40, text; 41–[45], note by Price headed 'To the Reader' on p. 41; [46], blank; [47], colophon; [48], blank.

Paper: wove, watermarked 'CURTIS RAG'; thickness 0.16 mm (pp. 17–18); total bulk 4.0 mm; brownish white; uncoated smooth.

Box: *material*: coarse calico, brownish gray. *Stamping*: gold. *Front*: 'PRESENCE | AND | ABSENCE'. *Spine and back*: unstamped. *Edges*: all edges cut and unstained. Unsewn signatures laid into a fall-down-back box lined with brownish gray laid paper. Also laid in are cardboard stiffeners in colors that vary from copy to copy.

Notes: No information about this item could be obtained from the publisher. It is certain, however, that publication was in 1974 (though the title page reads '1973'). $45.00. The colophon states that the edition is limited to 300 copies, but according to Price there were many overruns.
   Page [1] reads: 'This edition has been limited to three hundred copies, | of which two hundred and fifty copies are for sale. | This copy is number [arabic numerals in black fountain pen] | And is here signed by the Translator | [Price's signature in black fountain pen]'. Page [47] reads: 'The text of *Presence and Absence: Versions from the Bible* | by Reynolds Price was composed in Monotype Perpetua | and printed by The Press of A. Colish, Mount Vernon, New York | on Curtis Rag paper. | The format was designed by Andor Braun.'

A14 *A Nativity from the Apocryphal Book of James* 1974
(Christmas Greeting)

First Edition: [Reproduction of Rembrandt etching] | [the following words are a reproduction of Price's handwriting] A nativity from the Apocryphal Book of James / translated for | Christmas 1974

Copyright Page: none; the copyright notice is at the foot of p. [2].

Collation: 126 × 177 mm: [1²]; [1–4]. A single sheet folded once on a vertical axis.

Contents: [1], title page; [2–3], text; [4], reproduction of part of the etching from the title page and colophon.

Typography: 15 lines (p. [3]); 73 × 127 mm; 10 lines = 47 mm; face 2.5 (1.67x) mm. All printing is in brown ink.

Paper: wove unwatermarked; thickness 0.36 mm (pp. [1–2]); total bulk 0.72 mm; outer side brown, inner side white; uncoated smooth.

Notes: published 15 December 1974. Not for sale. 225 copies.
   Page [4] reads: 'This first printing of a Nativity from the | Apocryphal Book of James in a translation by | Reynolds Price is for his friends, at Christmas 1974. | The Virgin and Child with Saint Joseph is by Rembrandt. | Printed by David Southern at the Rooster Press.'

A15a   *The Surface of Earth*   1975

First edition: REYNOLDS | PRICE | [swelled rule] | THE | SURFACE | OF | EARTH | NEW YORK | ATHENEUM | 1975

Copyright Page: 'Parts of this novel appeared, in earlier forms, in | *Esquire, Harper's, Shenandoah, Southern Voices,* | and *The Virginia Quarterly Review.* | Copyright © 1973, 1974, 1975 by Reynolds Price | All rights reserved | Library of Congress catalog card number 74–32615 | ISBN 0–689–106–629 | Published simultaneously in Canada by McClelland & Stewart Ltd | Manufactured in the United States of America by H. Wolff, New York | Designed by Harry Ford | First Edition'.

Dedication Page: 'FOR | CHRISTOPHER BEEBE | AND | WILLIAM SINGER'.

Collation: 236 × 152 mm; [1–16¹⁶]; [i–xiv], [1–3] 4–18 [19] 20–25 [26] 27–32 [33] 34–50 [51] 52–75 [76] 77–87 [88] 89–98 [99] 100–123 [124–127] 128–148 [149] 150–173 [174] 175–244 [245] 246–275 [276] 277–288 [289] 290–316 [317–319] 320–382 [383] 384–403 [404] 405–441 [442] 443–448 [449] 450–491 [492–498].

Contents: [i–iii], blank; [iv], list of books by Price; [v], half title; [vi], blank; [vii], title page; [viii], copyright page; [ix], dedication page; [x], blank; [xi], table of contents; [xii], blank; [xiii], epigraph from Augustine's *Confessions*; [xiv], blank; [1]–491, text; [492], blank; [493], biographical note headed 'REYNOLDS PRICE'; [494–498], blank.

Running Titles: *head*: '[titles of books in italics, e.g., *'The Heart in Dreams'*] | [titles of chapters in italics, e.g., *'May 1921'*]'.

Typography: 45 lines (p. 202); 188 (196) × 114 mm; 10 lines = 41 mm; face 2.67 (1.67x) mm.

Paper: wove unwatermarked; thickness 0.15 mm (pp. 273–274); total bulk 39 mm; yellowish white; uncoated smooth.

Casing: *material*: calico, dark red. *Stamping*: gold. *Front*: 'REYNOLDS PRICE'. *Spine*: '[vert.] REYNOLDS PRICE | [horiz.] [swelled rule] | [vert.] THE SURFACE OF EARTH ATHENEUM'. *Back*: unstamped. *Edges*: all edges cut; top edge stained brownish red. *Endpapers*: wove unwatermarked; thickness 0.19 mm; dark yellow; uncoated smooth. *Bands*: head and tail bands have alternating stripes of red and yellow.

Jacket: total measurement 243 × 575 mm; wove unwatermarked paper; thickness 0.11 mm; inner side uncoated smooth; outer side coated glossy; inner side is white; front and flaps are white; lettering and decorations are brown, red, brownish yellow, yellow, green, and black. *Front*: '[on a white background] [brown] REYNOLDS PRICE | [red] THE SURFACE | OF EARTH | [black] A N O V E L | [painting by Price of the earth in cross section in green, yellow, brownish yellow, brown, and red]'. *Spine*: '[on a black background] [vert.] [yellow] REYNOLDS PRICE [brownish yellow] THE SURFACE OF EARTH | [horiz.] [yellow] ATHENEUM'. *Back*: '[black-and-white photo of Price, bled off all four sides]'. *Front flap*: '$10.95 | THE SURFACE OF EARTH | [46 lines principally roman, blurb] | *Jacket design: Reynolds Price* | *Jacket Photograph: Thomas Victor*'. *Back flap*: 'REYNOLDS PRICE | [54 lines principally roman, blurbs and quotes from reviews for LHL, NFH, GM, L&W, PE, and TT]'.

Notes: published 14 July 1975. $10.95. First printing of 15,000 copies.
   Photocopied page proofs of SOE were issued in advance of formal publication; they are bound in dark blue wrappers and have a white paper label, printed in red and black, pasted on the front. The label gives a tentative publication date of 23 May 1975.
   Atheneum has published two trade printings of SOE: first printing, June 1975; second printing, August 1975, with textual alterations to adjust the chronology of the novel.
   Atheneum has also published an offset replating in paperback (1981) of the second printing, with further textual corrections by Price.
   The copyright page of the first British "edition" (London: Arlington

Books) reads "*First published 1977 in England*" but a communication from Emma Glover of Arlington to West, 28 June 1979, states that formal publication was on 27 February 1978. The Arlington "edition" is an offset replating of the second Atheneum printing, priced at £7.50. The casing is light plum imitation cloth, the jacket deep plum lettered in bright orange and white. The press run was 10,000 copies. There has been one edition of SOE subsequent to the first:

A15b   New York: Avon Books, 1976. xii, 596 pp. Avon 29306. $1.95. Wrappers. Published November 1976.

A16   *Annunciation* (Christmas Greeting)   1975

First Edition: [Reproduction of Blake drawing] | [the following words are a reproduction of Price's handwriting] Annunciation | Christmas 1975

Copyright Page: none; the copyright notice is on p. [4].

Collation: 177 × 126 mm: [1²]; [1–4]. A single sheet folded once on a vertical axis.

Contents: [1], title page; [2–3], text; [4], oval-shaped reproduction of a woman's head by Blake and colophon.

Typography: 17 lines (p. [3]); 82 × 97 mm; 10 lines = 48 mm; face 2.67 (2.0x) mm. All printing is in brownish red ink.

Paper: wove unwatermarked; thickness 0.45 mm (pp. [3–4]); total bulk 0.90 mm; light brown; uncoated rough.

Notes: published 15 December 1975. Not for sale. 225 copies.
    Page [4] reads: 'This first printing of Annunciation by Reynolds Price | is for his friends, at Christmas 1975. | The angel and the woman are by William Blake. | Printed by David Southern. | © Reynolds Price 1975'.

A17   *The Good News According to Mark*   1976
                (Christmas Greeting)

First Edition: The Good News | According to Mark | T R A N S -
LATED BY | REYNOLDS PRICE | 1976

Copyright Page: 'Copyright © 1976 by Reynolds Price'.

Collation: 206 × 130 mm: fair bound; [1–6] 7–9 [10] 11–50 [51–56].

Contents: [1–2], blank; [3], half title; [4], blank; [5], title page; [6], copyright page; 7–9, untitled prefatory note by Price; [10], blank; 11–50, text; [51–52], blank; [53], statement of limitation and colophon; [54–56], blank.

Typography: 35 lines (p. 19); 160 × 85 mm; 10 lines = 45 mm; face 2.67 (1.67x) mm.

Paper: laid, chainlines 31 mm apart; watermarked '*Wausau Text*'; thickness 0.15 mm (pp. 21–22); total bulk 4.3 mm; brownish white; uncoated smooth.

Wrappers: two states; priority as follows: *State* 1: thickness 0.27 mm; both sides uncoated smooth; brownish white; lettering and decorations in red and black. *Front*: '[red lettering over a positive image of the Holy Shroud of Turin] The Good News | According to Mark | T R A N S - LATED BY | REYNOLDS PRICE'. *Spine*: '[against a red background] [black] THE GOOD NEWS ACCORDING TO MARK / translated by Reynolds Price'. *Back*: '[negative image of the Holy Shroud of Turin]'. *Edges*: all edges cut and unstained. *Endpapers*: two endpaperlike leaves have been inserted before p. [1] and after p. [56]; the leaves are of the same stock as the text but are dark orange rather than brownish white in color. *State* 2: lacks the "endpapers." The publisher notes: "Because of a binder's error about 20 copies were received without the colored endpapers. These were among the last bound and the binder had run out of the chosen paper." (Jack Shoemaker to West, 4 May 1979.)

Notes: published 15 November 1976. Three hundred copies were printed, of which 250 were distributed to friends by Price. The remaining 50 copies were numbered and signed by Price and sold by the publisher at $15.00 apiece to bookdealers. There were 11 additional copies: the printer and designer each kept three, and the publisher kept five. (Jack Shoemaker to West, 4 May 1979.)

Page [53] reads: 'There are three hundred copies of this first printing | of The Good News According to Mark | in a translation by Reynolds Price | for his friends, at Christmas 1976. | The face of Jesus—positive & negative images—|is from a photograph of the Holy Shroud of Turin. | Designed & typeset by George Mattingly, | printed at The West Coast Print Center, | & produced for the translator by Jack Shoemaker.'

A18   *Early Dark*   1977

First Edition: REYNOLDS PRICE | [swelled rule] | EARLY DARK | A PLAY | N E W   Y O R K | ATHENEUM | 1 9 7 7

Copyright Page: 'Professionals and amateurs are hereby | warned that EARLY DARK, being fully protected under | the Copyright Laws of the United States of Amer-|ica, the British Empire, including the Dominion of | Canada, and all other countries of the Berne and | Universal Copyright Conventions, is subject to | royalty. All rights, including profes-sional, amateur, | motion picture, recitation, lecturing, public reading, | radio and television broadcasting, and the rights of | translation into foreign languages, are strictly re-|served. Particular emphasis is laid on the question of | readings, permission for which must be secured from | the author's agent in writing. All inquiries should be | addressed to the author's agents, Russell and Volken-|ing, Inc., 551 Fifth Avenue, New York, N.Y. 10017. | Library of Congress Cataloging in Publication Data | Price, Reynolds, 1933– | Early dark. | I. Title. | PS3566.R54E3 1977 812'.5'4 77–3189 | ISBN 0–689–10799–4 | Copyright © 1977 by Reynolds Price | All rights reserved | Published simultaneously in Canada by McClelland and | Stewart Ltd | Manufactured by American Book–Stratford Press, Inc., | Saddle Brook, New Jersey | Designed by Harry Ford | First Edition'.

Dedication Page: 'F O R | KATHLEEN & HARRY FORD'.

Collation: 202 × 126 mm: [1–5¹⁶]; [2], [i–vii] viii–ix [x–xi] xii, [1–3] 4–12 [13] 14–16 [17] 18–20 [21] 22–51 [52–55] 56–73 [74–75] 76–78 [79] 80–97 [98–101] 102–111 [112–113] 114–129 [130–131] 132–135 [136–137] 138–140 [141–146].

Contents: [1], blank; [2], list of books by Price; [i], half title; [ii], blank; [iii], title page; [iv], copyright page; [v], dedication page; [vi], blank; [vii]–ix, preface by Price; [x], blank; [xi]–xii, list of characters in the play; [1]–140, text; [141–142], blank; [143], biographical note headed 'REYNOLDS PRICE'; [144–146], blank.

Running Titles: *head*: 'Early Dark | [act number in italics, e.g., 'Act One']'.

Typography: 34 lines (p. viii); 154 (160) × 84 mm; 10 lines = 44 mm; face 2.67 (1.67x) mm.

Paper: wove unwatermarked; thickness 0.135 mm (pp. 71–72); total bulk 11 mm; yellowish white; uncoated smooth.

Casing: *material*: calico, green. *Stamping*: gold. *Front*: 'REYNOLDS PRICE'. *Spine*: '[vert.] REYNOLDS PRICE | [horiz.] [swelled rule] | [vert.] EARLY DARK ATHENEUM'. *Back*: unstamped. *Edges*: all edges cut; top edge stained blue. *Endpapers*: wove unwatermarked: thickness 0.18 mm; dark blue; uncoated smooth.

Jacket: two states, differentiated by lettering on the spine. Priority as follows: *State* 1: total measurement 208 × 491 mm; wove unwatermarked paper; thickness 0.13 mm; inner side uncoated smooth; outer side coated glossy; inner side is white; back and flaps are white; front and spine are printed in light blue, maroon, and dark blue background panels; lettering is maroon, dark blue, and reversed out in white. *Front*: '[reversed out in white] [against a light blue panel] REYNOLDS | PRICE | [heavy white rule] | [against a maroon panel] E A R L Y | D A R K | [heavy white rule] | [against a dark blue panel] A PLAY'. *Spine*: '[horiz.] [heavy white rule] | [vert.] [reversed out in white] [against a maroon panel] EARLY DARK | [horiz.] [heavy white rule] | [vert.] [continuing in white] [against a dark blue panel] A PLAY ATHENEUM'. *Back*: '[maroon] *About THE SURFACE OF EARTH (1975)* | [dark blue] A *Novel by Reynolds Price* | [maroon] [8 lines principally roman, quote from a review] **Robert Ostermann**, *The National Observer* | [blue] [10 lines roman, blurb] **Eudora Welty** | [maroon] [6 lines principally roman, quote from a review] | **Allan Gurganus**, *Washington Post Book World* | [blue] [7 lines principally roman, blurb] **Howard Moss** | [maroon] [4 lines principally roman, quote from a review] | **George Cohen**, *Chicago Tribune Book World* | [blue] [7 lines roman, blurb] **Lord David Cecil**'. *Front flap*: '[blue] ISBN 0–689–10799–4 [38 mm separation] $7.95 | [maroon] REYNOLDS PRICE | EARLY DARK | [blue] [16 lines roman, quotation from Price's preface] | [7 lines roman, publisher's blurb]'. *Back flap*: '[maroon] REYNOLDS PRICE | [blue] [35 lines principally roman, blurbs and quotes from reviews for LHL, NFH, GM, L&W, PE, and TT] | [maroon] [rule] | For a note on the author, see the back of the book.' *State* 2: identical to State 1 except for the spine, which reads: '[vert.] [reversed out in white] [against a light blue panel] REYNOLDS PRICE | [horiz.] [heavy white rule] [the remainder of the spine is identical to the spine of State 1]'.

Notes: published 25 July 1977. $7.95. First printing of 3,000 copies.
 Proof copies of ED were issued by Atheneum in brownish yellow wrappers printed in black. Not seen.
 Atheneum has published only one impression of ED. There has been no British publication, nor has there been an edition of ED subsequent to the first.

A19   *Oracles* (Limited Signed Edition)   1977

First Edition: [red] ORACLES | [black] Six Versions from the Bible | by Reynolds Price | With etchings by Jacob Roquet | [seal of Duke University] | Durham | The Friends of Duke University Library | 1977

Copyright Page: 'Text Copyright © 1977 by Reynolds Price | Etchings Copyright © 1977 by Jacob Roquet'.

Collation: 231 × 145 mm: [1⁸ 2⁶ 3⁸]; [1–40]; etchings tipped in following pp. [8], [12], [18], [22], [26], [32]; the initial leaf of the first gathering and the final leaf of the last gathering are the front and back pastedown endpapers.

Contents: [1–4], blank; [5], title page; [6], copyright page; [7–35], text; [36], blank; [37], statement of limitation and colophon; [38–40], blank.

Typography: 25 lines (p. [15]); 160 × 102 mm; 10 lines = 62 mm; face 3.0 (2.0x) mm.

Paper: text is laid unwatermarked, chainlines 28.5 mm apart; thickness 0.18 mm (pp. [7–8]); yellowish white; uncoated rough; etchings are on two papers: (1) laid, chainlines 29 mm apart; watermarked 'CM | FABRIANO'; thickness 0.15 mm; brownish white; uncoated rough; (2) laid, chainlines 27 mm apart; watermarked '[griffin] | PERVSIA'; brownish white; uncoated rough; total bulk of text and etchings 4.5 mm.

Casing: *material*: calico, red. *Stamping*: gold. *Front and back*: an interlocking design within a light-rule box, the whole within a heavy-rule box. *Spine*: 'ORACLES'. *Edges*: all edges cut and unstained. *Endpapers*: as noted in the collation formula, the initial leaf of the first gathering and the final leaf of the last gathering function as the front and back pastedown endpapers; the second leaf of the first gathering and the next-to-last leaf of the last gathering therefore function as the front and back free endpapers.

Notes: published October 1977. $35.00. 300 copies with etchings, 6 without etchings.

Page [37] reads: 'ORACLES is published in an edition of | 300 copies each signed and numbered by | the translator and illustrator. 250 are for | public sale. The volume was designed & | printed by Wesley B. Tanner & produced | by Jack Shoemaker. The binding pattern | is based on a thirteenth century mosaic | in the Church of S. Giovanni battista in | Florence. The production of this book | was made possible by a grant from the | Mary Duke Biddle Foundation. No. [arabic numeral in black ink] | [Price's signature in black ink] | [Roquet's signature in black ink]'.

Six out-of-series copies of *Oracles*, lacking the tipped-in etchings, were hand-illustrated in black ink by Price himself; his drawings appear on the versos of pp. [8], [12], [18], [22], [26], and [32]. On the title page of each of the six copies, Price had struck through the line 'With etchings by Jacob Roquet' and has substituted 'with drawings by Reynolds Price' in black ink; he has also numbered each copy ('1/6', '2/6', '3/6', etc.) beneath the Duke University seal. Copy no. 1, on which the other copies are based, is at the Rare Book Room, Duke University Library.

A20 *Lessons Learned* (Limited Signed Edition) 1977

First Edition: [Bluish gray] Lessons | Learned | [black] *seven poems by* | [bluish gray] Reynolds Price | [black] ALBONDOCANI PRESS : NEW YORK : 1977

Copyright Page: '© Copyright 1972, 1973, 1977 by Reynolds Price | "At the Gulf" first appeared in *American Review* 17; an early form of "To | My Niece" in *The Southern Review*. The other five poems were previously | unpublished.'

Collation: 209 × 152 mm; [1^{12}]; [1–6] 7–19 [20–24].

Contents: [1–2], blank; [3], title page; [4], copyright page; [5], table of contents; [6], blank; 7–19, text; [20], blank; [21], statement of limitation and colophon; [22], 'Printed by William & Raquel Ferguson | Cambridge, Massachusetts | Albondocani Press Publication No. 22'; [23–24], blank. This collection of poems contains "Angel," "At the Gulf," "Wednesday, June the Sixth," "Leaving the Island," "Attis," "Anniversary," and "To My Niece: Our Photograph, in a Hammock."

Typography: 29 lines (p. 14); 144 (186) × approx. 105 mm; 10 lines = 48 mm; face 2.67 (1.67x) mm.

Paper: laid unwatermarked, chainlines 26 mm apart; thickness 0.18 mm (pp. 5–6); total bulk 2 mm; yellowish white; uncoated rough.

Sewn Wrappers: wove unwatermarked paper; thickness 0.57 mm; black; uncoated smooth.

Sewn Jacket: total measurement 214 × 480 mm; laid paper, chainlines 26 mm apart; inner side yellowish white; outer side marbled in bluish gray and orange; yellowish white paper label measuring 59 × 49 mm pasted on front 22 mm from top and 20 mm from spine, label printed in bluish gray as follows: '[within a single-rule box] Lessons | Learned | seven poems by | Reynolds Price'.

Notes: published 21 December 1977. $20.00. 226 copies. Four overrun copies, out of series, also signed by Price.
  Page [21] reads: 'This first edition of | LESSONS LEARNED | published in December 1977 | is limited to | two hundred and twenty-six copies. | The type is Palatino, | the paper is Antique Laid, | and the hand-sewn wrappers are | a French marble paper. | Two hundred copies | numbered 1–200 are for sale. | Twenty-six copies | lettered A–Z for the use | of the author and publisher | are not for sale. | All copies are signed | by the author. | This is number | [arabic numerals written in red ballpoint pen] | [Price's signature in black fountain pen]'.

A21   *The Dream of a House* (Broadside)   1977

First Edition: Recto: '[red] THE DREAM OF A HOUSE | [black] [text of poem in two columns] | [red] REYNOLDS PRICE | [Price's signature in black fountain pen]'.

Verso: '*THE DREAM OF A HOUSE by Reynolds Price | was designed and set in Centaur type by Richard Murdock | and is printed in an edition of 126 copies. | 100 numbered copies are for sale | and 26 lettered copies are for distribution. | This is copy* [arabic numeral in black fountain pen] | Palaemon Broadside Number Two | Copyright © 1977 by Reynolds Price'.

Collation: 390 × 260 mm: broadside.

Typography: 39 lines left col., 38 lines right col.; 249 (282) × 199 mm; 10 lines = 62 mm; face 2.5 (1.5x) mm.

Paper: wove unwatermarked; thickness 0.37 mm; white; uncoated rough.

Notes: published 22 December 1977. $10.00. 126 copies.
　　When the versos of *The Dream of a House* were first run through the press, the line 'Palaemon Broadside Number Two' was omitted. Fifteen of the twenty-six lettered copies, with the line missing, were given to Price, who signed and distributed them. The remaining lettered copies, and all 100 of the numbered copies, were run through the press again and the missing line was struck in.

A22   *A Palpable God*   1978

First Edition: REYNOLDS PRICE | [swelled rule] | A PALPABLE | GOD | THIRTY STORIES TRANSLATED FROM THE BIBLE | WITH AN ESSAY ON THE ORIGINS | AND LIFE OF NARRA-TIVE | N E W Y O R K | ATHENEUM | 1 9 7 8

Copyright Page: 'Library of Congress Cataloging in Publication Data | Price, Reynolds, 1933– | A palpable God. | Includes bibliographical references. | 1. Bible stories, English. 2. Story-telling—| History. I. Title. | BS550.2.P73 1978   220.9'505   77–10613 | ISBN 0–689–10837–0 | *Twenty of these versions, in early forms, were pub-lished in limited editions by Bruccoli Clark and by | The Friends of Duke University Library.* THE GOOD | NEWS ACCORDING TO MARK *was published privately | as a Christmas greeting. Early forms of others have | appeared in* SHENANDOAH *and* THE SAINT ANDREWS | REVIEW. *Thirteen appear here for the first time.* | Copyright © 1970, 1972, 1973, 1974, 1976, 1977, |

1978 *by Reynolds Price* | *All rights reserved* | *Published simultaneously in Canada by* | *McClelland and Stewart Ltd* | *Manufactured by American Book–Stratford Press, Inc.,* | *Saddle Brook, New Jersey* | *Designed by Harry Ford* | *First Edition'.*

Dedication Page: 'F O R | KATHERINE LAIRD ELLIS | NICHOLAS MICHAEL JORDAN | KATHERINE REYNOLDS PRICE | A N D | MARIE ELIZABETH PRICE'.

Collation: 203 × 127 mm: [1–4^{16} 5^8 6–7^{16}]; [2], [i–ix] x, [1–3] 4–46 [47] 48–60 [61–63] 64 [65] 66 [67–68] 69 [70] 71 [72] 73 [74] 75 [76] 77–78 [79–80] 81 [82] 83–86 [87–88] 89 [90] 91 [92] 93 [94] 95 [96] 97–98 [99–101] 102 [103] 104 [105] 106–107 [108] 109–110 [111] 112 [113] 114–115 [116] 117 [118] 119–120 [121] 122–123 [124–125] 126–147 [148] 149–191 [192] 193–195 [196].

Contents: [1], blank; [2], list of books by Price; [i], half title; [ii], blank; [iii], title page; [iv], copyright page; [v], dedication page; [vi], blank; [vii], epigraph from King James Version of the Bible; [viii], blank; [ix]–x, table of contents; [1], half title; [2], blank; [3]–195, text; [196], biographical note headed 'REYNOLDS PRICE'.

Running Titles: head: '[titles of versions in italics] | [titles of versions in italics]'.

Typography: 33 lines (p. 83); 148 (155) × 84 mm; 10 lines = 44 mm; 2.5 (1.5x) mm.

Paper: wove, watermarked '[arching arrangement of letters in first line] WARREN'S | OLDE STYLE'; thickness 0.15 mm (pp. 131–32); total bulk 16 mm; brownish white; uncoated smooth.

Casing: material: calico, light green. *Stamping:* gold. *Front:* 'REYNOLDS PRICE'. *Spine:* '[vert.] REYNOLDS PRICE | [horiz.] [swelled rule] | [vert.] A PALPABLE GOD ATHENEUM.' *Back:* unstamped. *Edges:* all edges cut; top edge stained pinkish red. *Endpapers:* wove unwatermarked; thickness 0.22 mm; dark orange; uncoated smooth.

Jacket: total measurement 493 × 206 mm; wove unwatermarked paper; thickness 0.14 mm; inner side uncoated smooth, outer side coated glossy; inner side and flaps are white; front, spine, and back are cream; lettering and decorations are in orange and black. *Front:* '[orange] REYNOLDS PRICE | [swelled rule] | A PALPABLE GOD | Thirty Stories Translated from the Bible | With an Essay on the Origins | and Life of Narrative | [black] [reproduction of an etching by Rembrandt]'. *Spine:* '[vert.] [orange] REYNOLDS PRICE   A PALPABLE GOD | [horiz.] [black] ATHENEUM'. *Back:* '[black] C O M M E N T   O N |

[orange] A PALPABLE GOD | [black] [10 lines roman, blurb] **Frank Kermode** | [9 lines roman, blurb] | **Professor W.D. Davies** | *The Divinity School, Duke University* | [8 lines roman, blurb] **Guy Davenport**'. *Front flap*: '[black] ISBN 0–689–10837–0 [40 mm separation] $8.95 | R E Y N O L D S P R I C E | [orange] A PALPABLE GOD | [black] [27 lines principally roman, description of the book, with a blurb by Frederick Buechner] | [orange] Jacket front: Rembrandt, Christ at Emmaus, 1654'. *Back flap*: '[black] R E Y N O L D S P R I C E | [orange] [27 lines ital, biographical note]'.

Notes: published 17 February 1978. $8.95. First printing of 4,000 copies.

Page proofs of PG, fair bound in brownish yellow paper wrappers, were issued in advance of publication; the front of the wrapper is printed in black and reads: 'REYNOLDS PRICE | [swelled rule] | A PALPABLE | GOD | THIRTY STORIES TRANSLATED FROM THE BIBLE | WITH AN ESSAY ON THE ORIGINS | AND LIFE OF NARRATIVE | [handwritten in black ink] ISBN: 0–689–10837–0 | [continuing in print] Pub. date: [rule] [handwritten in black ink above the rule is the date 'Feb. '78'] [continuing in print] Price: [rule] | [rule] | Unrevised proofs. Confidential. Please do not quote | for publication until verified with finished book. | N E W Y O R K | ATHENEUM | 1978'. Only fifteen copies of this advance PG were issued.

Atheneum has published only one impression of PG. There has been no British publication, nor has there been an edition subsequent to the first.

"The Easter Story" from PG has been reprinted in the *Detroit News Magazine*, 26 March 1978, p. 19.

A23   *Dead Man, Dying Girl* (Broadside)   1978

First Edition: *Recto*: '[left side] [brownish red] Dead Man, Dying Girl | [black] ROBERT KENNEDY 1925–1968 | [28 lines, principally roman, text of poem] | REYNOLDS PRICE | [Price's signature in black fountain pen] | [right side] [brownish red illustration of a woman's head, signed 'Chuck Miller' in black fountain pen] | [continuing in black] This poem, illustrated by Chuck Miller, is printed by Wesley B. Tanner on paper handmade | by the Imago Paper Mill. The edition of 200 numbered and 26 lettered copies is signed by the | poet and artist. Published by Phosphenes in April 1978. Copyright © 1978 by Reynolds Price. | This is number [letters or arabic numerals in black fountain pen]'.

Verso: blank.

Collation: 426 × 492 mm: broadside.

Typography: 32 lines, text page; 224 (292) × 118 mm; 10 lines = 70 mm; face 3.33 (2.0x) mm.

Paper: wove unwatermarked; thickness 0.27 mm; brownish white; uncoated rough. The bottom edge is an uncut or "deckle" edge.

Note: published 15 April 1978. 200 copies numbered ($15.00 retail); 26 copies lettered ($25.00 net); 30 copies imprinted 'Presentation Copy' (not for sale). (Gary M. Lepper to West, 29 April 1979.)

A24   *Pure Boys and Girls* (Broadside)   1978

First Edition: Recto: '[brown] Pure Boys and Girls | [black] [text of poem] | [brown] Reynolds Price | after Catullus XXXIV | [Price's signature in red ink]'.

Verso: '*This is copy* | [arabic numerals in black ink] | *Pure Boys and Girls* © 1978 by Reynolds Price'.

Collation: 328 × 247 mm: broadside.

Typography: 21 lines, text page; 220 (274) × 182 mm; 10 lines = 102 mm; face 4.5 (3.5x) mm.

Paper: wove unwatermarked; thickness 0.55 mm; gray; uncoated rough.

Notes: published 14 November 1978. Price of entire folio $125.00. 78 copies.
    Pure Boys and Girls is part of a broadside folio entitled *for Aaron Copland*; the colophon for the entire folio is printed on a separate stiff sheet 0.18 mm thick and reads: 'for Aaron Copland | *on the occasion of his seventy-eighth birthday* | 14 *November 1978* | This broadside folio is issued by Palaemon Press Limited | as the personal tribute of the publisher. | Seventy-eight sets, each containing an original poem by | James Dickey, Reynolds Price, and Robert Penn Warren, | and a specially commissioned woodcut by | Ann Carter Pollard, have been prepared and laid into hand-made folios. Fifty sets, numbered 1–50, | are for public sale, and twenty-eight sets, | numbered *i–xxvii*, are for the use of Mr. Copland, the | poets, the artist, and the publisher. Fourteen | lettered proof copies of the woodcut, out of series, have | been struck by the artist for her personal use. | This is number | [numbering in red ink]'. The folio itself is handmade; 347 × 275 mm; Cotlin spine; Swedish marbled paper-covered boards; brown cloth tapes.

A25   *Christ Child's Song at the End of the Night*   1978
                     (Christmas Greeting)

First Edition: [Self-wrappers] CHRIST CHILD'S SONG | AT THE END OF THE NIGHT | BY REYNOLDS PRICE | [drawing of an angel's head]

Copyright Page: '*Copyright* © 1978 *by Reynolds Price*'. The verso of the front self-wrapper is the copyright page.

Collation: 169 × 117 mm: [1²]; [1–4].

Contents: two states, no priority: *State 1*: [1], 'HOLIDAY GREET-INGS | AND | BEST WISHES | FOR THE | COMING YEAR'; [2–3], text of song; [4], statement of limitation. *State 2*: page [1] reads: 'HOLIDAY . . . YEAR | FROM | ALBONDOCANI PRESS | AND | AMPERSAND BOOKS'.

Typography: approx. 19 lines (pp. [2–3]); 113 × 75 mm; 10 lines = 56 mm; face 2.5 (1.5x) mm.

Paper: wove; watermarked 'RIVES'; thickness 0.18 mm (pp. [1–2]); total bulk 0.36 mm; brownish white; uncoated smooth.

Stapled Self-Wrappers: wove unwatermarked; thickness 0.31 mm; red; uncoated rough. The fore edge of the front of the self-wrapper and the fore edge of the first leaf of text are uncut or "deckle" edges. Issued in a white envelope with manila cardboard stiffener.

Notes: published 19 December 1978. Not for sale. 410 copies printed, 255 of State 1 and 155 of State 2.
    Page [4] reads: '*This first edition of* | CHRIST CHILD'S SONG AT | THE END OF THE NIGHT | *published in December 1978* | *is limited to* | *four hundred copies* | *to be used* | *as a holiday greeting* | *by the author and publisher.* | *None are for sale.* | Cover drawing by Robert Dunn | *Printed by* | *William Ferguson* | *for* | *Albondocani Press*'.

A26   *For Leontyne after* Ariadne (Broadside)   1979

First Edition: Recto: '[green] For Leontyne after *Ariadne* | [black] (San Francisco, 1977 – New York, 1979) | [three lines ital, epigraph from Hofmannsthal] | [text of poem] | [green] REYNOLDS PRICE'.

Verso: '[green] *100 copies of this poem* | *for Leontyne Price* | *were printed in March 1979.* | *This is number* [arabic numerals in green ink] | [Price's signature in green ink] | *Copyright* © 1979 *by Reynolds Price*'.

Collation: 304 × 228 mm: broadside.

Typography: 20 lines, text page; 175 (236) × 83 mm; 10 lines = approx. 85 mm; face 3.0 (2.33x) mm.

Paper: laid, chainlines 14 mm apart; watermarked '[script] Classic Text | [device]'; thickness 0.30 mm; light gray; uncoated smooth.

Note: published 5 April 1979. Not for sale. 105 copies.

A27   *The Lines of Life* (Broadside)   1979

First Edition: Recto: '[red] THE LINES OF LIFE | [black] —*after* Hölderlin | [four lines roman, text of poem] | Reynolds Price | [Price's signature in black fountain pen] | Eight copies have been privately printed for Stuart Wright; | six are lettered for presentation to his students, and two, num-|bered I and II, are for the translator. LAVS DEO! 8 June 1979. | Copyright © 1966 by Reynolds Price | [letters or roman numerals in black fountain pen]'.

Verso: blank.

Collation: 203 × 255 mm: broadside.

Typography: 4 lines, text page; 46 (131) × 150 mm; 10 lines = approx. 124 mm; face 5.0 (3.33x) mm.

Paper: wove unwatermarked; thickness 0.40 mm; white; uncoated rough.

Notes: published 8 June 1979. Not for sale. 8 copies.
For the first publication of this poem, see **C51**.

A28   *Question and Answer* (Pamphlet)   1979

First Edition: [Self-wrappers] Question and Answer | The Second | ARCHIBALD YELL SMITH IV LECTURE | *by* | REYNOLDS PRICE | [seal of The Baylor School] | *at* | The Baylor School | Chattanooga, Tennessee | April 26, 1979

Copyright Page: 'Copyright © 1978, 1979 by Reynolds Price'. The verso of the front wrapper is the copyright page.

Collation: 220 × 143 mm: [1⁶]; [1] 2–12.

Contents: [1], information about Smith Lecture; 2–11, text of Price's lecture; 12, biographical note on Price.

Typography: 36 lines (p. 4); 168 (181) × 100 mm; 10 lines = 46 mm; face 2.5 (1.5x) mm.

Paper: wove unwatermarked; thickness 0.13 mm (pp. 5–6); total bulk 0.79 mm; white; uncoated smooth.

Stapled Self-Wrappers: wove unwatermarked; thickness 0.23 mm; white; uncoated smooth. Printed in black on front recto and verso, which function respectively as title and copyright pages.

Note: published 1 Dec. 1979. Not for sale. 500 copies.

A29   *Nine Mysteries* (Limited Signed Edition)   1979

First Edition: [black] REYNOLDS | PRICE | [rule] | [red] NINE | MYS-TERIES | [black] (Four Joyful, Four Sorrowful, | One Glorious) | [original colored-pencil drawing by Price] | Palaemon Press

Copyright Page: 'Seven of these poems have appeared in earlier forms | in The Carolina Quarterly, The Ontario Review, | the second Archibald Smith IV Memorial Lecture, | and as private Christmas greetings. "Sleeping Wife" | and "Instruction" are first published here. | Copyright © 1975, 1978, 1979 by Reynolds Price'.

Collation: 244 × 172 mm: [1–4⁴]; [2], [1–6] 7–29 [30–34]. See *Notes* below.

Contents: [1–2], blank; [1], half title; [2], blank; [3], title page; [4], copyright page; [5], table of contents; [6], blank; 7–29, text; [30], blank; [31], statement of limitation; [32–34], blank. This collection of poems contains "Annunciation," "Reparation," "Christ Child's Song at the End of the Night," "Dead Girl," "Naked Boy," "Sleeping Wife," "Resurrection," "Instruction," and "Ascension."

Typography: 37 lines (p. 18); 182 (196) × approx. 80 mm; 10 lines = 49 mm; face 2.5 (1.67x) mm.

Paper: wove, watermarked '[script] Arches' parallel with the fore edge, which is deckle; thickness 0.19 mm (pp. 17–18); total bulk of pp. [1]–[32] 3.17 mm; grayish white; uncoated rough.

Binding: material: boards are linen, slate gray; spine is calf, black. *Stamping:* gold. *Front and back:* unstamped. *Spine:* 'NINE MYSTER-IES [leaf ornament] REYNOLDS PRICE'. *Edges:* unstained; top and fore edges cut, bottom edge deckle. *Endpapers:* wove unwatermarked; thickness 0.21 mm; grayish white; uncoated rough. The verso of the front free endpaper reads on the upper left-hand corner: 'HARCOURT BINDERY, BOSTON'. See *Notes* below.

Notes: published 15 December 1979. $200.00. First printing of 20 copies.

Page [31] reads: "This first edition of *Nine Mysteries* is limited to | 309 signed copies. Nine specially bound copies, each | with a drawing by the author, are lettered A–I. | *Christmas 1979* | [Price's signature in maroon ink]'.

The binder wrapped an extra sheet of paper, identical in stock to the endpapers, around all four signatures of the first printing before affixing the special binding. Thus there is one extra blank leaf between the front free endpaper and the half title and another between p. [32] and the back free endpaper. These two extra leaves are conjugate with one another. Properly speaking these are binder's leaves and not part of the signatures, but they must be figured into the page count of the book.

Only twenty copies of the first printing survive. Nine are the specially bound copies described above. All remaining copies of the first printing were misbound. Ten of these misbound copies were sent to the publisher and one to Price. When the binding error was discovered, all other copies, save these eleven, were destroyed.

A second printing of 307 copies was published 1 February 1980 at $20.00. This printing is in effect the trade "edition." Copies can be identified by the following points: (1) no colored-pencil drawing by Price on the title page; (2) the text paper of both printings is of identical stock, but in the second printing the watermark is parallel with the fore edge, which is deckle, and the top and bottom edges are cut; (3) the casing is entirely in black calico with gold-stamping on the spine identical to that of the special binding but with a blind-stamped numeral '9' measuring 28 mm in height on the front of the casing; the endpapers are wove unwatermarked; thickness 0.23 mm; red; uncoated rough; (4) the casing of the second printing is approximately 3 mm shorter and 1 mm wider than the special binding of the first printing; (5) there is no extra wraparound "endpaper" in the second-printing copies.

"Sleeping Wife" and "Instruction," here first published, are rept. in *Ontario Review*, no. 13 (Fall-Winter 1980–1981), 27–31. Both poems are collected in VP.

A30   *Socrates and Alcibiades* (Broadside)   1980

First Edition: *Recto*: '[red] Socrates and Alcibiades | [black] —*after* Hölderlin | [text of poem] | [red] Reynolds Price | [Price's signature in red ink] | LIMITED TO SEVENTY-FIVE NUMBERED COPIES OF WHICH THIS IS NUMBER [arabic numerals in red ink] | COPYRIGHT © 1980 BY REYNOLDS PRICE'.

Verso: blank.

Collation: 354 × 228 mm: broadside.

Typography: 8 lines, text page; 75 (172) × approx. 95 mm; 10 lines = approx. 80 mm; face 3.5 (2.0x) mm.

Paper: wove, watermarked 'BFK RIVES'; thickness 0.36 mm; grayish white; uncoated rough.

Notes: published 24 April 1980 (by Palaemon Press). Price of entire folio $250.00. 75 copies, numbered 1–75.

Socrates and Alcibiades is part of a broadside slipcased folio entitled *RPW* 24•IV•80, a tribute to Robert Penn Warren on his 75th birthday. The colophon for the entire folio is printed on a separate stiff sheet 0.18 mm thick and reads: '[black] FOR ROBERT PENN WARREN [red] ~ [black] 24•IV•80 [red] ~ [black] OF SEVENTY-|FIVE SETS PUBLISHED, FIFTY-FIVE ARE FOR PUBLIC SALE. | FIFTEEN ADDITIONAL COPIES OF THE WOODCUT ARE FOR | THE USE OF THE ARTIST. THIS IS SET NO. [arabic numerals in red ink]. | [Wright's signature in black ink] | [continuing in black] . . . *wer kann aber auch einem grossen Dichter genug dan-|ken, dem kostbarsten Kleinod einer Nation?*—|Ludwig van Beethoven to Bettina von Arnim, April 1811'. The inner part of the slipcase is of unfinished grayish-green buckram; the outer case has English marbled boards in light and dark green (10 copies in a marbled paper that is green, pale orange, red, and grayish pink, no priority of papers); the spine is covered in the same grayish-green buckram as above, with a gold-leaf rule separating spine and boards at all points; the slipcase measures 366 × 236 mm. Besides the broadside by Price, the folio includes a woodcut by Ann Carter Pollard and broadside poems by A. R. Ammons, Fred Chappell, James Dickey, Richard Eberhart, George Garrett, John Hollander, William Meredith, Rosanna Warren, and Richard Wilbur.

A31   *The Annual Heron* (Limited Signed Edition)   1980

First Edition: [Blue] *The Annual Heron* | [black] *by* | [blue] *Reynolds Price* | [black] ALBONDOCANI PRESS: NEW YORK: 1980

Copyright Page: '*Copyright* © 1979 *by Reynolds Price* | First appeared in *Poetry* December, 1979.'

Collation: 203 × 152 mm: [1^{10}]; [1–20].

Contents: [1–2], blank; [3], title page; [4], copyright page; [5], half title; [6], blank; [7–15], text; [16], blank; [17], statement of limitation and colophon; [18], 'Printed by NADJA/New York | Albondocani Press Publication No. 26'.

Typography: 28 lines (p. [9]); 137 × approx. 80 mm; 10 lines = 49 mm; face 3.0 (2.0x) mm.

Paper: laid unwatermarked, vert. chainlines 27 mm apart; thickness 0.18 mm (pp. [19–20]); total bulk 1.85 mm; brownish white; uncoated rough.

Sewn Wrappers: wove unwatermarked paper; thickness 0.26 mm; black; uncoated rough.

Sewn Jacket: total measurement 210 × 495 mm; marbled paper, laid with chainlines 26 mm apart; watermarked '[four letters within an oval] LANA INGREW [three words within another oval] MADE IN | FRANCE'; inner side grayish white; outer side marbled in black, blue, red-orange, and yellow-orange; white paper label measuring 62 × 50 mm pasted on front 25 mm from top and 20 mm from spine, label printed in black as follows: '[within a heavy-rule rectangle] *The Annual Heron* | *by* | *Reynolds Price*'.

Notes: published 17 December 1980. $30.00. 300 numbered copies only, all signed, 100 given to Price for distribution, 200 for sale. Price's copies were selected from throughout the numbering (he received no two copies with consecutive numbers), and therefore there are no "author" numbers as opposed to "publisher" numbers.

Page [17] reads: *'This first edition of* | THE ANNUAL HERON | *published in December 1980* | *is limited to* | *three hundred numbered copies* | *of which two hundred are for sale.* | *The type is Baskerville,* | *the paper is Michelangelo,* | *and the hand-sewn wrappers are* | *a French marble paper.* | *All copies are signed* | *by the author.* | *This is number* | [numerals in red ink] | [Price's signature in blue ink]'.

A32   A *Final Letter* (Limited Signed Edition) 1980 [1981]

First Edition: [Within a double-rule rectangle 137 × 84 mm, the outer rule slightly heavier than the inner rule, the entire area within the rectangle printed first in yellowish brown with lettering over in black] REYNOLDS PRICE | A | Final Letter | *Robinson Mayfield* | *in Essex, North Carolina* | *to* | *Hutchins Mayfield* | *in Oxford, England* | *June 15 to November 27,* | 1955 | SYLVESTER & OR-PHANOS | LOS ANGELES CALIFORNIA | 1980

Copyright Page: 'Copyright © 1980 by Reynolds Price'.

Collation: 218 × approx. 139 mm: [1–2⁸ 3⁴ 4⁸]; [i–viii], 1–41 [42–48].

Contents: [1–2], blank; [3], half title; [4], blank; [5], title page; [6], copyright page; [7], prefatory note by Price; [8], blank; 1–41, text; [42], blank; [43], statement of limitation and colophon; [44–48], blank.

Typography: 24 lines (p. 35); 134 (146) × 84 mm; 10 lines = 56 mm; face 3.33 (2.0x) mm.

Paper: wove, watermarked '[script] Arches' parallel with the fore edge, which is deckle; thickness 0.20 mm (pp. 1–2); total bulk 5.65 mm; brownish white; uncoated rough.

Casing: *material*: coarse calico, brown. *Stamping*: black and gold. *Front*: the initials 'R | P', each 22 mm high, in black within a gold rectangle 60 × 51 mm, the whole enclosed within a black rectangular box 73 × 64 mm, the sides of which are 6 mm thick. The black stamping was done first as a solid block 73 × 64 mm; the gold then was stamped over in a block 60 × 51 mm with the initials dropped out; the final effect is of the black rectangular box recessed into the front of the casing, the gold rectangle further recessed, and the black initials raised from the gold. *Spine*: black paste-on rectangle 136 × 8.5 mm with lettering and decorations in gold: '[ornament] A FINAL LETTER • PRICE [ornament]'. *Back*: unstamped. *Edges*: unstained; top and bottom edges cut, fore edge deckle. *Endpapers*: laid, vert. chainlines 26 mm apart; watermarked '[script] Arches'; thickness 0.19 mm; brownish white; uncoated rough. *Bands*: yellow and blue headband and tailband.

Notes: published 6 February 1981. $50.00 for numbered copies. 330 copies (300 numbered, 26 lettered, 4 with the printed name of a recipient), plus 30–35 out-of-series copies imprinted 'PRESENTATION COPY' on the colophon page for distribution by Price and the publishers.

Page [43] reads: 'PUBLISHED BY | STATHIS ORPHANOS & RALPH SYLVESTER | IN A LIMITED EDITION OF 330 COPIES. | THREE HUNDRED ARE NUMBERED, | TWENTY-SIX LETTERED, AND FOUR BEAR | THE PRINTED NAME OF A RECIPIENT. | THE TEXT IS SET IN JANSON TYPES, | THE PAPER IS ARCHES MOULD-MADE. | ALL COPIES ARE SIGNED BY THE AUTHOR. | DE-SIGNED BY GRANT DAHLSTROM | AND PRINTED AT THE | CASTLE PRESS. | [Price's signature in black ink]'.

According to the publisher, the 26 lettered copies will not be sold or distributed, at least for the present. These copies were all enclosed in plain black calico openfaced slipcases after publication.

The four copies with the printed name of a recipient went to Price, Harriet Wasserman (Price's agent), Stathis Orphanos, and Ralph Sylvester.

A Final Letter is an excerpt from *SL*.

A33   *The Source of Light*   1981

First Edition: REYNOLDS | PRICE | [swelled rule] | | THE | SOURCE | OF | LIGHT | N E W   Y O R K | ATHENEUM | 1 9 8 1

Copyright Page: 'Parts of this novel appeared, in earlier | forms, in AN-
TAEUS and in a limited edition | from SYLVESTER & ORPHANOS. | Library
of Congress Cataloging in Publication Data | Price, Reynolds, 1933– |
The source of light. | I. Title. | PS3566.R54S6   1981   813'.54   80–
69650 | ISBN 0–689–11136–3 | Copyright © 1980, 1981 by Reynolds
Price | All rights reserved | Published simultaneously in Canada by
McClelland and Stewart Ltd | Manufactured by American Book–Strat-
ford Press, | Saddle Brook, New Jersey | Designed by Harry Ford | First
Edition'.

Dedication Page: 'F O R | DAVID CECIL | A N D | STEPHEN
SPENDER'.

Collation: [1–8¹⁶ 9⁸ 10–11¹⁶]; [i–xii], [1–3] 4–153 [154–157] 158–261
[262–265] 266–318 [319–324].

Contents: [i], blank; [ii], list of books by Price; [iii], half title; [iv], blank;
[v], title page; [vi], copyright page; [vii], dedication page; [viii], blank;
[ix], table of contents; [x], blank; [xi], epigraph from Swedenborg; [xii],
blank; [1], divisional half title; [2], blank; [3]–153, text of Book One;
[154], blank; [155], divisional half title; [156], blank; [157]–261, text of
Book Two; [262], blank; [263], divisional half title; [264], blank; [265]–
318, text of Book Three; [319–320], blank; [321], biographical note
headed 'REYNOLDS PRICE'; [322–324], blank.

Typography: 44 lines (p. 44); 185 (193) × 113 mm; 10 lines = 41 mm;
face 2.5 (1.5x) mm.

Paper: wove unwatermarked; thickness 0.14 mm (pp. 167–68); total
bulk 23 mm; yellowish white; uncoated smooth.

Casing: *material*: calico, brown. *Stamping*: gold. *Front*: 'REYNOLDS
PRICE'. *Spine*: '[vert.] REYNOLDS PRICE | [horiz.] [swelled rule] |
[vert.] THE SOURCE OF LIGHT ATHENEUM'. *Back*: unstamped.
Edges: all edges cut; top edge stained pinkish red. *Endpapers*: wove
unwatermarked; thickness 0.17 mm; yellowish white; uncoated
smooth.

Jacket: total measurement 240 × 560 mm; wove unwatermarked paper; thickness 0.14 mm; inner side is white, uncoated smooth; outer
side is white, coated glossy; lettering and decorations are in dark green,
light green, dark yellow, orange, and black. *Front*: '[on a dark green
background completely covering the front and spine] [dark yellow] The
| Source | of Light | [light green] A NOVEL BY | [orange] Reynolds |
Price | [light green] AUTHOR OF | A *Long and Happy Life* and *The
Surface of Earth*'. *Spine*: '[vert.] [dark yellow] The Source of Light

[orange] Reynolds Price | [horiz.] [light green] ATHENEUM'. *Back*: '[black-and-white photo of Price, 89 mm in height, bled off top and sides] | [dark green] Photograph by Thomas Victor | [orange] NOV-ELS BY REYNOLDS PRICE | [dark green] THE SURFACE OF EARTH (1975) | [black] [6 lines roman, blurb by Howard Moss] | [dark green] LOVE AND WORK (1968) | [black] [6 lines roman and ital, quote from a review by Vernon Scannell in the *New States-man*] | [dark green] A GENEROUS MAN (1966) | [black] [2 lines roman, blurb by Allen Tate] | [dark green] A LONG AND HAPPY LIFE (1962) | [black] [3 lines roman and ital, quote from a review by Honor Tracy in the *New Leader*]'. *Front flap*: '[orange] ISBN 0-689-11136-3 $13.95 | [dark green] [6 lines roman and ital, blurb] | [black] [36 lines roman and ital, description of SL] | [dark green] [6 lines roman and ital, blurb] | [orange] Jacket design copyright © 1981 by Paul Bacon'. *Back flap*: '[orange] OTHER BOOKS | BY REYN-OLDS PRICE | [40 lines, roman and ital, dark green and black, blurbs and quotes from reviews of NFH, PE, TT, ED, and PG]'.

Notes: published 23 April 1981. $13.95. First printing of 10,000 copies.

Fifty advance copies bound in yellow wrappers were issued. These copies consist of 306 pages of photocopied proofs, with page numbers handwritten in the margins of the original proofs from which the photocopies were made. The front reads: 'REYNOLDS | PRICE | [swelled rule] | THE | SOURCE | OF | LIGHT | [16 typed lines giving a probable publication date of April 1981 and a probable price of $12.95] | NEW YORK | ATHE-NEUM | 1981'. The Atheneum catalog description of the novel is repro-duced on p. [iii].

Atheneum has to date published one trade printing of SL: first printing, April 1981.

Excerpts from this novel were prepublished in A32 and C142.

A "copy" of SL in unsewn gatherings was sent to the Rare Book Depart-ment, Perkins Library, Duke University. These gatherings are signed on the spine of each gathering so that the signatures are covered by the casing. Signing is: 'THE SOURCE OF LIGHT – SIG 1 – PGS A, B, I–X, 1–20–', etc.

A34   *Country Mouse, City Mouse* (Pamphlet)   1981

First Edition: [On the front wrapper, against a black-and-white photo-graph of a corner drugstore and pedestrians] [violet] Country Mouse, | City Mouse | [decorative rule] | Reynolds Price

Copyright Page: none; the copyright notice is on p. [8].

Collation: 208 × 136 mm; [1⁴]; [1–8].

Contents: [1], 'Country Mouse, | City Mouse | [decorative rule] | Reynolds Price'; [2], in black within a violet rectangle measuring 174 × 94 mm, a 16-line note by Price on the previous publication of this item; [3–7], text; [8], copyright notice, statement of limitation, and colophon, all in black within a violet rectangle measuring 174 × 94 mm.

Typography: 34 lines (p. [4]); 176 × 95 mm; 10 lines = 51 mm; face 2.33 (1.5x) mm.

Paper: wove unwatermarked; thickness 0.16 mm (pp. [1–2]); total bulk 0.68 mm; gray; uncoated rough.

Stapled Wrappers: total measurement 222 × 143 mm; wove unwatermarked paper; thickness 0.19 mm; white; uncoated smooth.

Notes: published October 1981. Not for sale. 500 copies, 50 of which were numbered and signed.
     Page [8] reads: 'Copyright 1981 Reynolds Price | ISBN: 0–933598–02–5 | Published by the Friends of the Library, | North Carolina Wesleyan College | on the occasion of Mr Price's reading, | 11 october 1981, | in an edition of five-hundred. | Fifty are numbered and signed. | [number in black ink] | [Price's signature in black fountain pen] | *Country Mouse, City Mouse* | was designed and typeset at | Bull City Studios, | and printed and bound at the | Regulator Press, | Durham, North Carolina. | The cover photograph was made | April 20, 1947 at the corner of Main and | Front Streets, Burlington, North Carolina | by Charles Cooper, and is reprinted with the | permission of the *City-County Newspaper* | of Burlington.'

A35 A *Start* (Limited Signed Edition) 1981

First Edition: [black] REYNOLDS | PRICE | [rule] | [red] A START | [black] (Early Work) | PALAEMON PRESS LIMITED

Copyright Page: 'Copyright 1981 by Reynolds Price'.

Collation: 251 × 152 mm: [1¹⁸]; [2], [i–ii], [1–2] 3–26 [27–32]. See *Notes* below.

Contents: [1–2], blank; [i–ii], blank; [1], title page; [2], copyright page; 3–6, Price's preface and his note on the text; 7–26, text; [27], statement of limitation; [28–32], blank. This collection of juvenilia contains "The Wise Men," "To Kay," "Emily Dickinson," "I Stood," "For Jane," "Cards," " 'Different,' " "To a Negro," "Never Imagined," "In Triumphant Gray Procession," "Afternoon," "And This Is Symbol," "On Watching a College Student Reading Chapman's Homer," and "Because I Am."

Typography: 36 lines (p. 22); 177 (186) × 92 mm; 10 lines = 47 mm; face 2.5 (1.67x) mm.

Paper: wove, watermarked '[script] Arches' parallel with the fore edge; thickness 0.19 mm (pp. 7–8); total bulk of pp. [i–30] 3.26 mm; brownish white; uncoated smooth.

Binding: *material*: boards are marbled paper; two papers, no priority: *Paper 1* is brown, white, brownish yellow, and orange with the marbling arching upward toward the top edge; *Paper 2* is black, brown, white, brownish yellow, and red with the marbling arching toward the fore edge; spine is medium brown calf. *Stamping*: gold. *Front and back*: unstamped. *Spine*: 'A START — PRICE PALAEMON'. *Edges*: unstained; all edges uncut. *Endpapers*: identical to text paper; see *Notes* below.

Notes: published 30 December 1981. $150.00. 83 copies, of which 75 were bound. Two of the unbound copies were used for copyright purposes.

Page [27] reads: 'THIS EDITION IS LIMITED TO | SEVENTY-FIVE NUMBERED COPIES. | [number by Price] | [signature by Price, both number and signature in black fountain pen]'.

The binder wrapped an extra sheet, identical in stock to the single 16-leaf signature of the book, around that signature before stitching. The two extra leaves thus created are the front and back pastedown endpapers. Properly speaking these are binder's leaves, but they are sewn in with the single gathering and thus are figured into the total page count. Pages [i–ii] and [29–30] function as the front and back free endpapers.

A36   *Vital Provisions*   1982

First Edition: REYNOLDS | PRICE | [swelled rule] | VITAL | PROVI-SIONS | NEW YORK | ATHENEUM | 1982

Copyright Page: 'Some of these poems appeared, in earlier forms, in the following places: | ALBONDOCANI PRESS *Angel, Anniversary, Archaic Torso of Apollo,* | *Christ Child's Song at the End of the Night, Leaving the Island* | THE AMERICAN REVIEW *At the Gulf* | THE ARCHIVE *Black Water* | THE CAROLINA QUARTERLY *Man and Faun, Naked Boy* | EN-COUNTER *I Say of Any Man* | THE GEORGIA REVIEW *Divine Propositions* | THE MASSACHUSETTS REVIEW *The Dream of Lee* | THE ONTARIO REVIEW *Ascension, Reparation, Resurrection, Seafarer* | PALAEMON PRESS *The Dream of a House, Instruction, Pure Boys* | *and Girls, Sleeping Wife* | PERMANENT ERRORS *The Alchemist* | POETRY *The Annual Heron, Pictures of the Dead, Rescue* | PRIVATE GREETINGS AND A BROADSIDE *Annunciation, Cumaean Song, For* | *Leontyne Price after Ariadne* | QUES-TION AND ANSWER *Dead Girl* | SOUTHERN REVIEW *Bethlehem—Cave of the Nativity, Jerusalem—Calvary,* | *To My Niece* | Library of Congress Cataloging in Publication Data | Price, Reynolds, 1933– | Vital provisions. | I. Title. | PS3566.R54V5 1982 811'.54 82–71255 | ISBN 0–689–11322–6 | ISBN 0–689–11323–4 (pbk.) | Copyright © 1982 by Reynolds Price | All rights reserved | Published simultaneously in Canada by McClelland and Stewart Ltd | Composed and printed by Heritage Printers, Inc., | Charlotte, North Carolina | Bound by The Delmar Company, Charlotte, North Carolina | Designed by Harry Ford | First Edition'.

Dedication Page: a poem appears on what would normally be the dedication page: 'ANGEL | [9 lines italic]'.

Collation: 234 × 143 mm: [1–7⁸]; [i–xiv], [1–2] 3–34 [35–36] 37–57 [58–60] 61–93 [94–98].

Contents: [i–iii], blank; [iv], list of books by Price; [v], half title; [vi], blank; [vii], title page; [viii], copyright page; [ix], statement initialed 'R. P.' regarding the order of the poems in VP; [x], blank; [xi–xii], table of contents; [xiii], dedication page with poem; [xiv], blank; [1], divisional half title: 'ONE'; [2], blank; 3–34, text; [35], divisional half title: 'TWO | NINE MYSTERIES | *(Four Joyful, Four Sorrowful, One Glorious)*'; [36], blank; 37–57, text; [58], divisional half title: 'THREE'; [60], blank; 61–93, text; [94], blank; [95], biographical note headed 'REYNOLDS PRICE'; [96–98], blank.

Typography: 39 lines (p. 53); 180 (196) × approx. 70 mm; 10 lines = 46 mm; face 2.67 (1.67x) mm.

Paper: wove unwatermarked; thickness 0.16 mm (pp. 13–14); total bulk 9 mm; yellowish white; uncoated smooth.

Casing: *material*: calico, gray-blue. *Stamping*: gold. *Front*: 'REYNOLDS PRICE'. *Spine*: '[vert.] REYNOLDS PRICE | [horiz.] [rule] | [vert.] VITAL PROVISIONS ATHENEUM'. *Back*: unstamped. *Edges*: all edges cut, top edge stained bright blue. *Endpapers*: wove unwatermarked; thickness 0.16 mm; yellowish white; uncoated smooth.

Jacket: total measurement 241 × 529 mm; wove unwatermarked paper; thickness 0.145 mm; inner side uncoated smooth, outer side coated glossy; inner side is white; back and flaps of outer side are white, front and spine are light blue; all lettering and decorations in black, blue, and white. *Front*: '[on a blue panel, reversed out in white] VITAL | PROVISIONS | POEMS BY | REYNOLDS | PRICE | [gray-blue halftone, scene of a pond in winter]'. *Spine*: '[vert.] [reversed out in white] REYNOLDS PRICE VITAL PROVISIONS ATHE-

NEUM'. *Back*: '[blue] BOOKS BY REYNOLDS PRICE | [43 lines principally roman, blurbs and quotations from reviews for various Price titles, printed alternately in blue and black]'. *Front flap*: 'ISBN 0–689– 11322–6 $14.95 | [29 lines principally roman, description of book] | [blue] *Jacket photograph by Reynolds Price; design by | Harry Ford'*. *Back flap*: '[black-and-white photograph of Price] | [blue] *Photograph of Reynolds Price by Stathis Orphanos | For a note on the author see the back of the book'*.

> *Notes*: published 30 Nov. 1982. Issued simultaneously in cloth and paper. $14.95 cloth; $7.95 paper. First printing of 3,000; 1,000 cloth, 2,000 paper. Advance page proofs were issued in wrappers. Not seen.
> Atheneum has to date published one impression of VP. There has been no British publication.
> *Simultaneous Paperback Publication*: sheets are identical to those in the clothbound issue; fair bound; wrappers 0.30 mm thick; identical on front and spine to the dust jacket of the clothbound issue. *Back*: '[black-and-white photograph of Price in upper left-hand corner] ISBN 0–689–11323– 4 $7.95 | [copy from front flap of clothbound dust jacket] | [blue] *Cover photograph by Reynolds Price; design by Harry Ford | Photograph of Reynolds Price by Stathis Orphanos | For a note on the author see the back of the book'*.

A37 *Mustian* 1983

First Edition: REYNOLDS | PRICE | [swelled rule] | MUSTIAN | TWO NOVELS AND A STORY | COMPLETE AND UN- ABRIDGED | A GENEROUS MAN | A CHAIN OF LOVE | A LONG AND HAPPY LIFE | N E W Y O R K | ATHENEUM | 1983

Copyright Page: '[all lines centered] | Copyright © 1983 by Reynolds Price | All rights reserved | A LONG AND HAPPY LIFE | Copyright © 1960 by *Encounter*, Ltd. | Copyright © 1961 by Reynolds Price | A CHAIN OF LOVE copyright © 1963 by Reynolds Price | A GENEROUS MAN copyright © 1966 by Reynolds Price | Published simultaneously in Canada by McClelland and Stewart Ltd | ISBN 0–689–11377–3 | Library of Congress catalog card number 82–73009 | Manufactured by Fairfield Graphics, Fairfield, Pennsylvania | Designed by Harry Ford | First Edition'.

Dedication Pages: as in the original editions, reproduced by photo-offset.

Collation: 235 × 154 mm: [1–10^{16}]; [2], [i–v] vi–xiv [xv–xvi], [1–3] 4– 46 [47] 48–140 [141] 142–158 [159–161] 162–182 [183–185] 186–225 [226] 227–272 [273] 274–301 [302].

Contents: [1], blank; [2], list of books by Price; [i], half title; [ii], blank; [iii], title page; [iv], copyright page; [v]–xiv, preface by Price; [xv], table of contents; [xvi], blank; [1], divisional half title 'A GENEROUS | MAN'; [2], dedication page for GM; [3]–158, text of GM; [159], divisional half title 'A CHAIN OF LOVE'; [160], blank; [161]–182, text of "A Chain of Love"; [183], divisional half title 'A LONG | AND HAPPY | LIFE' [184], dedication page for LHL; [185]–301, text of LHL; [302], biographical note headed 'REYNOLDS PRICE'.

Typography: 43 lines (p. 23); 182 (188) × 105 mm; 10 lines = 42 mm; face 2.67 (1.5x) mm.

Paper: wove unwatermarked; thickness 0.13 mm (pp. 169–70); total bulk 21 mm; brownish white; uncoated smooth.

Casing: *material*: calico, black. *Stamping*: gold. *Front*: 'REYNOLDS PRICE'. *Spine*: '[vert.] REYNOLDS PRICE | [horiz.] [swelled rule] | [vert.] MUSTIAN ATHENEUM'. *Back*: unstamped. *Edges*: all edges cut, top edge stained red-orange. *Endpapers*: wove unwatermarked; thickness 0.16 mm; brownish white; uncoated smooth.

Jacket: total measurement 241 × 562 mm; wove unwatermarked paper; thickness 0.14 mm; inner side uncoated smooth, outer side coated glossy; inner side is white; flaps of outer side are white, front and spine are black, back is black-and-white photograph; lettering and decorations in yellow, orange, and black. *Front*: '[yellow] REYNOLDS | PRICE | [rule] | [orange] MUSTIAN | [yellow] [rule] | TWO NOVELS AND A STORY | COMPLETE AND UNABRIDGED | [rule] | A GENEROUS MAN | A CHAIN OF LOVE | A LONG AND HAPPY LIFE'. *Spine*: '[vert. in two lines] [yellow] REYNOLDS | PRICE | [horiz.] [rule] | [vert.] [orange] MUSTIAN | [horiz.] [yellow] [rule] | [vert.] ATHENEUM'. *Back*: black-and-white photograph of Price, bled off all edges. *Front flap*: ISBN 0–689–11377–3 $14.95 | [43 lines principally roman, description of book]'. *Back flap*: '[orange] REYNOLDS | PRICE | [black] [21 lines principally roman, biographical note] | [orange] *Photograph by Stathis Orphanos*'.

Notes: published 25 April 1983. $14.95. First printing of 4,000 copies, all clothbound.

Advance page proofs were issued in wrappers. Not seen.

Atheneum has to date published one impression of M. There has been no British publication.

Mustian was typeset by a Kurzweil Data Entry Machine (KDEM). The first-edition texts of the materials in *Mustian* were scanned by the machine and recorded on magnetic tape, which in turn was used to drive a photo-composition system. Thus the texts were rendered in a uniform type face and page design. The work was performed at Crane Typesetting Service, Barnstable, Massachusetts.

A38   *A Chain of Love* (Japanese Textbook)   [1984]

First Edition: Nan'un-do's Contemporary Library | [rule] | A CHAIN
OF LOVE | REYNOLDS PRICE | *EDITED WITH NOTES* | *BY* |
Tokiya Nakajima | Hisashi Saito | [rule] | Tokyo | NAN'UN-DO | [logo] |
C-P15

Copyright Page: 'Reprinted by permission of Russell & Volkening Inc.
| From *The Names and Faces of Heroes* by Reynolds Price. | © 1958,
1963 by Reynolds Price | © 1958, 1963 by Macmillan & Co. Ltd. |
English language textbook with Japanese annotations rights arranged |
through Charles E. Tuttle Company Inc., Tokyo'.

Collation: 181 × 126 mm: fair bound; [4], i–iv [v–vi], 1–71 [72] 73–
102 [103–104].

Contents: [1], title page; [2], copyright page; [3], tipped-in black-and-
white photo of Price on glossy paper 0.65 thick; [4] blank; i–iv, introduction, in a combination of English and Japanese; [v], table of contents; [vi], blank; 1–42, text of "A Chain of Love," in English; 43–71,
text of "The Anniversary," in English; [72], blank; 73–102, explanatory
notes and glosses, in a combination of English and Japanese; [103–
104], publication data and advertisements, in Japanese.

Typography: 27 lines (p. 38); 130 (138) × 85 mm; 10 lines = 47 mm;
face 2.0 (1.5x) mm.

Paper: wove unwatermarked; thickness 0.10 mm (pp. 31–32); total bulk
6.0 mm; yellowish white; uncoated smooth.

Wrappers: thickness 0.36 mm; outer side with coated pebbly finish;
inner side uncoated smooth; both sides white; lettering in black; rec-
tangles in light blue. Two white binding leaves, thickness 0.10, uncoated smooth, are included in the front of the book, and two are
included in the back. The first of these in the front, and the second of
these in the back, are pasted, along the fore edges only, to the inside
front wrapper and inside back wrapper respectively. *Front*: 'Nan'un-do's
Contemporary Library | [within a solid blue rectangle, 164 × 116 mm]
A CHAIN OF LOVE | REYNOLDS PRICE | Tokyo | NAN'UN-DO |
[logo] [outside the rectangle] C—P15'. *Spine*: '[on a white background]
R. PRICE A CHAIN OF LOVE [double elbow bracket opening right]
C-P15 [double elbow bracket opening left] NUD'. *Back*: '[within a solid
blue rectangle 164 × 114 mm] NUD [double elbow bracket opening
right] C-P15 [double elbow bracket opening left]'.

Note: exact publication date, price, and printing run unknown. Published
sometime in February 1984.

A39   *Private Contentment*   1984

First Edition: REYNOLDS | PRICE | [swelled rule] | PRIVATE | CON-
TENTMENT | A PLAY | N E W Y O R K | ATHENEUM | 1984

Copyright Page: 'CAUTION: *Professionals and amateurs are hereby* |
warned that PRIVATE CONTENTMENT, *being fully pro-|tected under the
Copyright Laws of the United States | of America, the British Empire,
including the Do-|minion of Canada, and all other countries of the* |
*Berne and Universal Copyright Conventions, is sub-|ject to royalty. All
rights, including professional, | amateur, motion picture, recitation, lec-
turing, public | reading, radio and television broadcasting, and the* |
*rights of translation into foreign language, are strictly | reserved. Partic-
ular emphasis is laid on the question | of readings, permission for which
must be secured | from the author's agent in writing. All inquiries* |
*should be addressed to the author's agent, Harriet | Wasserman Literary
Agency, Inc., 230 East 48 Street, New York City 10017. | Copyright ©
1984 by Reynolds Price | All rights reserved | Published simultaneously
in Canada by | McClelland and Stewart Ltd | ISBN 0-689-11455-9 |
Library of Congress catalog card number 83-45523 | Composition by
Heritage Printers, Inc., | Charlotte, North Carolina | Manufactured by
Fairfield Graphics, | Fairfield Pennsylvania | Designed by Harry Ford* |
First Edition'.

Dedication Page: ' F O R | JEFFREY ANDERSON'.

Collation: 203 × 127 mm: [1–5¹⁶]; [i–xvi], [1–3] 4–5 [6] 7 [8] 9 [10–
11] 12–19 [20] 21 [22] 23 [24] 25–30 [31] 32 [33] 34–40 [41] 42–45
[46] 47–55 [56] 57–66 [67] 68–69 [70–71] 72–78 [79] 80–95 [96] 97
[98] 99–105 [106] 107–115 [116] 117–118 [119] 120–132 [133] 134–
136 [137–144].

Contents: [i], blank; [ii], list of books by Price; [iii], half title; [iv], blank;
[v], title page; [vi], copyright page; [vii], dedication page; [viii], blank;
[ix], note by Price; [x], blank; [xi], list of characters in the screenplay;
[xii], blank; [xiii], 'PLACES | A *military base in Idaho and eastern
North Carolina* | TIME | *March* 1945'; [xiv], blank; [xv], note on the
first televised presentation of PC and the cast and credits for that production; [xvi], blank; [1], half title; [2], blank; [3]–136, text; [137–138],
blank; [139], biographical note headed 'REYNOLDS PRICE'; [140–
144], blank.

Typography: 32 lines (p. 17); 146 (151) × 85 mm; 10 lines = 45 mm;
face 2.5 (1.5x) mm.

Paper: wove unwatermarked; thickness 0.135 mm (pp. 61–62); total
bulk 11 mm; brownish white; uncoated smooth.

Casing: *material*: calico, raspberry. *Stamping*: gold. *Front*: 'REYN-OLDS PRICE'. *Spine*: '[vert.] REYNOLDS PRICE | [horiz.] [swelled rule] | [vert.] PRIVATE CONTENTMENT ATHENEUM'. *Back*: unstamped. *Edges*: all edges cut; top edge stained orange. *Endpapers*: wove unwatermarked; thickness o.16 mm; brownish white; uncoated smooth.

Jacket: total measurement 208 × 488 mm; wove unwatermarked paper; thickness o.15 mm; inner side uncoated smooth; outer side coated glossy; inner side is white; flaps are white; front, spine, and back are printed in black, white, and copper. *Front*: black-and-white halftone of four members of the television cast sitting at a piano; in the upper right corner, within a copper octagon, reversed out in white, is: 'PRIVATE | CONTENTMENT | A PLAY BY | REYNOLDS | PRICE'. *Spine*: printed vertically against a black background '[white] REYNOLDS PRICE [copper] PRIVATE CONTENTMENT [white] ATHENEUM'. *Back*: black-and-white halftone of Price, bled off all edges. *Front flap*: 'ISBN 0–689–11455–9 $12.95 | [33 lines principally roman, description of screenplay] | [copper] *Photograph on front of jacket courtesy Don Perdue | and American Playhouse: the original cast of Private | Contentment, John McMartin and Kathryn Walker above, | Trini Alvarado and Peter Gallagher below.*' *Back flap*: '[21 lines principally roman, biographical note] | [copper] *Photograph of Reynolds Price on back | of jacket by Stathis Orphanos*'.

Notes: published 26 March 1984. $12.95. First printing of 3,000 copies, all clothbound.

Atheneum has published only one impression of PC. There has been no British publication, nor has there been an edition of PC subsequent to the first.

B

Contributions to Books

B1   *Songs of Youth: Annual Anthology* (Los Angeles: American Poetry Society, 1950). First publication of Price's poem, "To Kay," on p. 96. In ringbound printed wrappers. No statement of first edition.

B2   *Winter's Tales 4* (London: Macmillan & Co. Ltd., 1958). First publication of "The Anniversary," on pp. 149–78 (rept. in **A2**, **A38**). Blue cloth, stamped in gold; printed dust jacket. No statement of first edition.

B3   *Light Blue, Dark Blue: An Anthology of Recent Writing from Oxford and Cambridge Universities*, ed. Julian Mitchell et al. (London: Macdonald, 1960). First book appearance of "A Chain of Love" (**C38**), on pp. 97–126. Blue cloth, printed in blue; printed dust jacket. 'First published in 1960' on copyright page.

B4   *Prize Stories 1961: The O. Henry Awards*, ed. Richard Poirier (Garden City, N.Y.: Doubleday, 1961). First book appearance of "One Sunday in Late July" (**C43**), on pp. 101–44. Black cloth, stamped in gold; printed dust jacket. 'First Edition' on copyright page.

B5   *Prize Stories 1962: The O. Henry Awards*, ed. Richard Poirier (Garden City, N.Y.: Doubleday, 1962). First book appearance of "The Warrior Princess Ozimba" (**C46**), on pp. 251–57. Pale tannish green cloth, stamped in light brown; printed dust jacket. 'First Edition' on copyright page.

B6   *The Young Writer at Chapel Hill: Number Five*, ed. Jessie Rehder (Chapel Hill: Dept. of English, Univ. of North Carolina, 1966). First publication of Price's descriptive note on Raphael Jones's story, "Ducks Don't Fly on a Cloudless Day," p. 4. In wire-stitched printed pictorial wrappers. No statement of first edition.

B7   *Chapel Hill Carousel*, ed. Jessie Rehder (Chapel Hill: Univ. of North Carolina Press, 1967). First book appearance of "A Long and Happy Life: Fragments of Groundwork" (**C61**), on pp. 173–85. Grayish blue cloth, stamped in gold; printed pictorial dust jacket. No statement of first edition.

B8   William Faulkner, *Pylon* (New York: The New American Library, 1968). First book appearance of Price's introductory essay (**C71**), on pp. v–xvii. Published as Signet Modern Classic CQ415. In printed pictorial wrappers. 'FIRST PRINTING, SEPTEMBER, 1968' on copyright page.

B9 Afterwords: Novelists on Their Novels, ed. Thomas McCormack (New York: Harper & Row, 1968). First book appearance of "News for the Mineshaft" (C73), on pp. 106–23. Dull orange and black cloth, stamped in gold and copper; printed pictorial dust jacket. 'FIRST EDITION' on copyright page.

B10 Henry James, The Wings of the Dove (Columbus, Ohio: Charles E. Merrill, 1970). First publication of the introduction by Price, "The Wings of the Dove—A Single Combat," on pp. v–xix (rept. in A10). In printed pictorial wrappers. No statement of first edition.
Note: This book was issued in wrappers only, although the copyright page calls for a cloth issue as well.

B11 Who's Who in America, 1970–71, 36 (Chicago: Marquis, 1970). First publication of Price's untitled statement in "World Figures Sum Up Their Aspirations," on p. xi (rept. in Contemporary Novelists, ed. James Vinson [London: St. James Press; New York: St. Martin's Press, 1976], p. 1109). Maroon cloth, stamped in gold; issued without dust jacket.

B12 Voices from Earth: A Collection of Writings on Environment, ed. James Applewhite [Greensboro, N.C., 1971]. First book appearance of "Man and Faun" (C75), on p. 30. In printed wrappers. No statement of first edition.

B13 The Current Voice: Readings in Contemporary Prose, ed. Don L. Cook et al. (Englewood Cliffs, N.J.: Prentice-Hall, 1971). Alternate edition. First book appearance of "Life for Life" (C65), on pp. 58–60. Printed pictorial cloth; no dust jacket. No statement of first edition.

B14 You Can't Magnolias, ed. H. Brandt Ayers and Thomas Naylor (New York: McGraw-Hill, 1972). First publication of Price's essay "Dodo, Phoenix, or Tough Old Cock," on pp. 71–81 (rept. in A10). Blue cloth, stamped in silver; printed pictorial dust jacket. 'First Edition' on copyright page.

B15 Writer's Choice, ed. Rust Hills (New York: David McKay, 1974). First publication of a long note by Price on the writing of "Waiting at Dachau" (C81) on pp. 309–11; the story is reprinted on pp. 313–37. Red cloth, printed in black; dust jacket. Also issued in printed wrappers. No statement of first edition.

B16 World Authors 1950–1970, ed. John Wakeman (New York: H. W. Wilson, 1975). First publication of a lengthy autobiographical statement by Price on pp. 1165–66. Orangish brown cloth, stamped in gold. No statement of first edition.

B17   A *Celebration of Art and Cookery*, ed. Beth Cummings Paschal
(Raleigh: North Carolina Art Society, 1976). First publication of
Price's contribution, "Mr. Gilliam's Johnnycake," on p. 60.
Deep tan pictorial cloth, printed in white; issued without dusk
jacket. No statement of first edition.

B18   *Self-Portrait: Book People Picture Themselves*, from the collection of Burt Britton (New York: Random House, 1976). First
publication of Price's self-portrait on p. 37. Black cloth and paper boards, stamped in gold; printed dust jacket. Also issued in
printed wrappers. '*First Edition*' on copyright page.

B19   *Duke Encounters*, ed. Elizabeth H. Locke (Durham: Duke University Office of Publications, 1977). Collection of personal
statements by alumni and faculty that "attempt to capture and
portray the spirit of Duke University." First publication of Price's
statement on p. 20. Blue cloth, stamped in gold; unprinted glassine dust jacket. Also issued in blue paper wrappers, stamped in
gold. No statement of first edition.
Note: Only a limited number of copies of the cloth issue were
prepared for contributors and special alumni and friends.

B20   *Contemporary Poetry of North Carolina*, ed. Guy Owen and
Mary C. Williams (Winston-Salem: John F. Blair, 1977). First
publication of Price's poem, "Angel," on p. 100 (rept. in **A36**).
Blue cloth, stamped in silver; printed dust jacket. No statement
of first edition.

B21   *Symbolism and Modern Literture: Studies in Honor of Wallace
Fowlie*, ed. Marcel Tetel (Durham: Duke Univ. Press, 1978).
First publication of Price's "Damon's Epigraph: A Translation of
Epitaphium Damonis by John Milton," on pp. 165–70. Light
blue cloth, stamped in gold; printed dust jacket. No statement of
first edition.

B22   *Eudora Welty: A Form of Thanks*, ed. Louis Dollarhide and Ann
J. Abadie (Jackson: University Press of Mississippi, 1979). First
publication of Price's "A Form of Thanks," on pp. 123–28; his
poem "To My Niece: Our Photograph, in a Hammock" (**C92**) is
reprinted on pp. 126–28. Tan cloth, printed in reddish brown
and dark brown; printed pictorial dust jacket. Also issued in
printed pictorial wrappers. No statement of first edition.

B23   Romulus Linney, *Jesus Tales* (San Francisco: North Point Press,
1980). First publication of the foreword by Price, on pp. xi–xiv.
Blue cloth, stamped in silver; printed dust jacket. No statement
of first edition.

B24   David Rhoads and Donald Michie, *Mark as Story: An Introduction to the Narrative of a Gospel*. (Philadelphia: Fortress Press, 1982). First publication of the foreword by Price, on pp. xi–xiii. Plum wrappers printed in black and white. No statement of first edition.

B25   *Eudora Welty: A Tribute* (Winston-Salem, N.C.: Printed for Stuart Wright, 1984). First publication of "From Reynolds Price (as of 13 April 1984)," pp. 17–20, a special birthday tribute to Eudora Welty. Seventy-five copies printed, of which fifty were issued in marbled-paper wrappers, twenty-three in quarter leather and marbled-paper boards, and two in full leather boards.

Note: This special 75th-birthday tribute to Eudora Welty includes contributions by Cleanth Brooks, Bernard Malamud, William Maxwell, Reynolds Price, William Jay Smith, Elizabeth Spencer, Peter Taylor, Anne Tyler, Robert Penn Warren, and Richard Wilbur; each tribute is signed by the author. Five numbered offprints of Price's contribution were prepared from overrun sheets.

C

Appearances in Periodicals

and Newspapers

C1   "Angels with Bows." *Hi-Times* (Broughton High School, Raleigh, N.C., student newspaper), 16 (13 Dec. 1949), 5. Story. Printed under the rubric "Scribbling Scribes."

This story of approximately 375 words is Price's debut in print. It is about six boys—"angels with bows on"—who go out for their church choir despite the anticipated taunting of their peers. "Strangely," Price concludes, "the front row boys did not laugh at all."

C2   "Younger Generation Not Vipers." *Hi-Times*, 16 (3 Feb. 1950), 6. Unsigned essay, the first of two to appear under the rubric "Price Says." See below, **C4**.

Price defends the youth of his generation, particularly his colleagues at Broughton High School, pointing to a certain civic consciousness that they display.

C3   "I dreamt that a woman fell into a slime." *News and Observer* (Raleigh, N.C.), 26 Feb. 1950, Sec. 4, p. 5. Unsigned poem.

Sam Ragan, editor of the "Southern Accent" column in which this poem appeared, wrote: " 'Perhaps our young people think more profoundly about Christ-like attitudes than we realize,' a teacher in the Raleigh schools writes. And, as evidence, she submits the following poem by a high school student which came across her desk a few days ago."
    A note on the front page of *Hi-Times*, 5 April 1950, states that a poem by Price, "Neither Do I Condemn Thee—Sin No More," appeared in Ragan's "Southern Accent" column on 5 March. This poem could not be located in that issue, nor in any issue four weeks before or after 5 March 1950.

C4   "Leave [Ingrid] Bergman Alone for Now." *Hi-Times*, 16 (3 March 1950), 6. Signed 'Reynolds Price / February 1950'. Published in the "Price Says" column.

C5   "Epilogue." *Hi-Times*, 16 (5 May 1950), 3. Poem.

C6   "Emily Dickinson." *News and Observer*, 21 May 1950, Sec. 4, p. 5. Poem.

Rept. in **A35**.

C7   "Editorial Policy." *Hi-Times*, 17 (6 Oct. 1950), 2. Signed "E. R. P."

C8   "Football Attitudes." *Hi-Times*, 17 (6 Oct. 1950), 2. Unsigned editorial by Price.

Price defends the game for the values inherent in it: "character growth, moral strength, and maturity of emotion." According to *Hi-Times*, 23 May 1951, football was Price's "preferred sport."

C9   "To the Seniors." *Hi-Times*, 17 (6 Oct. 1950), 2. Editorial signed "Reynolds Price."

C10   "The United Nations." *Hi-Times*, 17 (10 Nov. 1950), 2. Editorial signed "R. P."

C11   "On Teachers." *Hi-Times*, 17 (10 Nov. 1950), 2. Editorial signed "Reynolds Price."

C12   "Love Lyric." *Winged Words* (Broughton High School student literary magazine), 1 (Dec. 1950), [5]. Poem.

A note on the front page of the *Hi-Times*, 15 Dec. 1950, gives the proposed publication date of *Winged Words* as 18 December. The purpose of *Winged Words*, as explained in the *Hi-Times*, was "to recognize those students at Broughton who write well and those whose work is never seen." Also contained in this issue is an untitled story by Price. See below, C13.
    Rept. in **B1**.

C13   Untitled story. *Winged Words*, 1 (Dec. 1950), 10–12.

This story of approximately 300 words is about a girl who attempts to sell inexpensive greeting cards to the seated customers in a small-town drugstore. She says that she wants to buy her mother a birthday present. Some customers believe her, some do not. The young girl sells two (for a dime each), but "she wasn't as glad as she wanted to be. She didn't know why."
    Rept. in **A35** as "Cards."

C14   "A Child." *Hi-Times*, 17 (15 Dec. 1950), 2. Editorial signed "R. P."

This editorial and the one following (**C15**) demonstrate Price's early interest in the Bible: "The angel Gabriel had given to the girl this name [Jesus] when he came to her home in Nazareth of Galilee announcing to her that she was to bear the 'Son of the Highest.' He had said to the virgin, 'The Lord God shall give unto him the throne of his father David: and he shall reign over the house of Jacob forever; and of his kingdom there shall be no end.' The girl kept all these things and pondered them in her heart and knew that the child in her womb was the Son of God."

C15 "Christmas." *Hi-Times*, 17 (15 Dec. 1950), 2. Editorial signed "R. P."

"We have misplaced Christmas and made no attempt to find it. We have raised in place of its beautiful and sacred symbols, pretty figures of our own contriving—Santa Claus in place of Joseph, who took a girl named Mary when she was already with child and tenderly shielded her from the talk of small people. A snow Queen has been superimposed over the virgin herself, whom God chose of all women to bear his matchless gift. As for the Child whose day it is—He has been lost."

1951

C16 "Great Danish Tenor Meets Broughton Journalists." *Hi-Times*, 17 (1 Feb. 1951), 1, 4. Article.

Lauritz Melchior, who was to perform in Raleigh, was interviewed in his suite at the Sir Walter Raleigh Hotel by Price. The *Heldentenor* had just returned from an African safari. Melchior discussed his operatic debut, his most embarrassing moment, and his mutual love of opera and the cinema. Price concludes: "And perhaps not knowing it, Lauritz Melchior epitomized his whole forty-three-year career—'When you have a life you should have a full life.'"

C17 "Laughter and the Man." *Hi-Times*, 17 (1 Feb. 1951), 2. Editorial signed "R. P."

"Man will always laugh. He must laugh, or die from his fears. But he will laugh at what he chooses, and his choice is a crystal-clear reflection of his character."

C18 "Different." *Hi-Times*, 17 (1 Feb. 1951), 2. Story.

This story concerns a boy, Rep, who, after seeing the film "Cabin in the Sky," says he wants to be a "colored person." His friend John Walter is black. Rep asks, "Why can't I go to John Walter's school sometimes, Daddy? To colored school? And why can't he come with me sometimes? He'd sure like the underpass." "Because," his father replies, "John Walter is different."
Rept. in **A35**.

C19 "What Is Effective English Teaching?" *North Carolina English Teacher*, 8 (Feb. 1951), 3–4, 15. Panel discussion.

Price edited a panel discussion among members of the Wake County (N.C.) English Council and the Wake County College English Teachers. Price was a student representative and member of the panel. His comments are found on p. 15: "The effectiveness of English teaching is in direct ratio to the teacher's ability to bring students to the realization that English is life. The teacher must take his subject out of the classroom and into the world, for English is *not* a subject. It is life. So long as we remain heirs of the English heritage, whether we speak, think, act, see, or hear, we must use the English language—and we must employ it with accuracy, intelligence, and understanding."

C20   "On the Student Council Election." *Hi-Times*, 17 (6 April 1951), 2. Editorial signed "R. P."

C21   "Your Duty." *Hi-Times*, 17 (6 April 1951), 2. Editorial signed "R. P."

C22   "I weep to find the blue sea white." *Hi-Times*, 17 (4 May 1951), 2. Poem.

C23   "On Editing a Paper." *Hi-Times*, 17 (4 May 1951), 2. Editorial signed "Reynolds Price."

C24   "To the New Seniors." *Hi-Times*, 17 (23 May 1951), 2. Editorial signed "Reynolds Price."

"Some of you will cry, and some will laugh to keep from crying. Some will feel terribly alone in the midst of hundreds of people; others will be challenged by their future. A few will feel all these feelings and know as Browning knew 'Youth shows but half; trust God: see all, nor be afraid!'"

C25   "On the Timelessness of an Old Face." *Creative Writing* (Los Angeles), 2 (Oct. 1951), 21. Poem.

1953

C26   "Sacrament." *Archive* (Duke Univ. student literary magazine), 66 (Oct. 1953), 32. Poem.

1954

C27   "Shakespeare and the Divine Right of Kings." *Archive*, 66 (Feb. 1954), 4–6, 22. Essay.

C28   "*Vanity Fair*—a Personal Reaction." *Archive*, 66 (April 1954), 12–13. Essay.

C29   "In triumphant gray procession." *Archive*, 66 (April 1954), 13. Poem.

Rept. in A35.

C30 "In Defense . . . ." *Archive*, 67 (Oct. 1954), 2–3. Editorial signed "E. R. P."

"Ideally . . . the printed work should be of a quality which requires no justification. But THE ARCHIVE does draw on essentially imperfect writers, and I suppose that it would do no harm either to me or to you if I say briefly why these few pieces were chosen from the body of work submitted." Price was editor of *Archive* for the 1954–55 school year.

C31 "Cast a Warm Eye." *Archive*, 67 (Dec. 1954), 2–3. Editorial signed "E. R. P."

C32 "Michael Egerton." *Archive*, 67 (Dec. 1954), 17–19. Story.

One sentence was inadvertently omitted from the original publication of "Michael Egerton." It appears in all the republications as the third sentence from the end of the story: "I don't think he heard me."
  The Spring 1973 issue of the *Archive*, titled the *Trinity Archive*, is a special boxed set of four separate parts. Part 4, which contains "Michael Egerton," is entitled "ōld'ēz" and devoted to student work previously published in the *Archive*. Also included are pieces by James Applewhite, Fred Chappell, William Styron, and Anne Tyler.
  Rept. in *Country Beautiful*, 2 (Oct. 1962), as "The Ordeal of Michael Egerton," 32–35; **A2**; *Ten Modern American Short Stories*, ed. David A. Sohn (New York: Bantam Books, 1965), pp. 81–87 (Bantam Pathfinder Edition FP 113); *New Worlds of Ideas*, ed. Glenda Richter and Clarence Irving (New York: Harcourt, Brace, 1969), pp. 69–75; *Spectrum 2: Language, Literature, and Composition*, ed. Jay Cline et al. (Boston: Ginn and Co., 1969), pp. 199–204; *English Seventy*, ed. Anthony Chamberlin et al. (Stockholm: Bokförlaget Natur och Kultur, 1970), pp. 62–67; *Moments in Literature*, ed. Philip McFarland et al. (Boston: Houghton Mifflin, 1972), pp. 464–68; *Trinity Archive*, pt. 4, 85 (Spring 1973), 25–30; *To Be: Identity in Literature*, ed. Edmund J. Farrell et al. (Glenview: Scott, Foresman, 1976), 253–56.

1955

C33 "An Obedient Servant, But. . . ." *Archive*, 67 (Feb. 1955), 2–3. Unsigned editorial.

Price defends the position that the *Archive* should be allowed to publish "some distinguished piece by a generous writer outside this [Duke Univ.] community." The following issue (April 1955) did in fact contain the first publication of Eudora Welty's "Place in Fiction" as well as three of Welty's WPA photographs.

C34 "A Kind of Valedictory." *Archive*, 67 (April 1955), 2–3, 30–31. Editorial signed "E. R. P."

"When Eudora Welty visited this campus in February, someone asked her what she considered the great faults of student writing. Her reply was, I thought, keen in its simplicity. Paraphrasing a character in E. M. Forster's *Howards End*, she said that the trouble with *bad* student writing is the trouble with *all* bad writing. It is not serious, and it does not tell the truth.

That, to a large degree, is just it. Those students who *do* take time to write anything beyond term papers and letters home usually do not take *enough* time. Their stories, their sketches, their poems almost always suffer from the spectre of the deadline. The student has a story riding somewhere on the top of his mind for some time, not taking it too seriously; then with some chagrin he realizes that a deadline in his English class is fast approaching, and he sits at his typewriter and drains that story off the upper layer of his mind where it has rested—hardly nourished, hardly developed. He usually tells his conscience that now the deadline is met, after a fashion, he can return to the piece in leisure and develop it slowly and richly. But that seldom happens, and for two good reasons: the time is never found, and—most fatally—a story has a way of taking a life of its own—however premature and malformed—once it has been set to paper. It simply defies the normal writer to change it in any organic way. That is how a promising story often gets itself killed a-borning, in haste and in a failure of devotion. That is the trouble, the apparently irremediable trouble, with most student writing. There is no lack of things to say, and most of them are things worth saying and hearing; but there is a woeful lack of those who *can* say what they only dimly know."

Price wrote the headnotes for this issue of the *Archive* as well most of the others in 1954–55.

C35 "To Accompany John Nash's 'The Moat.'" *Archive*, 67 (April 1955), 29. Poem.

1957

C36 "Seeing, Loving, and Behaving Yourself." *Encounter*, 9 (Aug. 1957), 85–86. Review of Zoë Oldenbourg, *The Awakened*; Arthur Steuer, *The Terrible Swift Sword*; Albert Camus, *The Fall*; Henri de Montherlant, *Desert Love*; and Iris Murdoch, *The Sandcastle*.

C37 "A Review." *Postmaster* (Merton College, Oxford), 2 (Dec. 1957), 21–22. Review of an Oxford performance of *The Two Noble Kinsmen*.

1958

C38 "A Chain of Love." *Encounter*, 10 (March 1958), 3–17. Story.

Rept. with authorial revisions in **B3**; *Critic*, 21 (Oct./Nov. 1962), 41–42; *Under Twenty-five: Duke Narrative and Verse, 1945–1962*, ed. William Blackburn (Durham: Duke Univ. Press, 1963), pp. 205–35; **A2**; *A Time for Growing*, ed. Jean Van Leeuwen (New York: Random House, 1967), pp. 106–40; **A38**.

This number of *Encounter* contains a note by Price, partly autobiographical and partly concerned with the story, on p. 88.

1959

C39 "Art or African Violets?" *Concept* (Converse College, Spartanburg, S.C., student literary magazine), 59 (Jan. 1959), 12–13. Price's critique of student writing which had appeared in the preceding issue of *Concept* (vol. 59, no. 1).

C40 "The January Issue." *Concept*, 59 (March 1959), 14–15. Price's critique of student writing which had appeared in the preceding issue of *Concept* (vol. 59, no. 2).

C41 "Troubled Sleep." *Encounter*, 12 (April 1959), 3–9. Story.

A note by Price on the genesis of this story is printed on p. 96 of this number of *Encounter*.
Rept. in *Best Articles & Stories*, 4 (March 1960), 58–62, and in **A2**.

C42 "The Class of 1955 Newsletter." *American Oxonian* (official magazine of the Alumni Association of American Rhodes Scholars), 46 (Oct. 1959), 248. Contains a brief note by Price concerning his activities for the year (completing a volume of stories "to be called . . . A *Long and Happy Life* and to be published by Random House in late spring of '60") and his teaching of freshman and sophomore English at Duke two-and-a-half days a week (a "pretty ideal set up").

This is the first of fifteen such yearly contributions by Price to the *American Oxonian*. Others are in Vol. 49 (Oct. 1962), 302 (returns to Oxford to work on NFH and a novel in progress, GM); 50 (Oct. 1963), 258 (mentions GM); 51 (Oct. 1964), 233 (finishing GM, which he calls "freewheeling and comic"); 52 (Oct. 1965), 258 (mentions screenplay for LHL); 53 (Oct. 1966), 251 (his pleasure in the creation of GM, just published); 54 (July 1967), 212 (NEA grant and work on a second volume of stories); 55 (July 1968), 194 (back in England working on L&W); 56 (July 1969), 193 (hard at work on the new book of stories); 58 (July 1971), 186 (lecturing and reading around the country, PE, and work on a book of essays); 59 (July 1972), 180 (mentions TT); 60 (July 1973), 139 (mentions "The Heart in Dreams"); 61 (July 1974), 165 (mentions SOE); 62, no. 2 (1975), 131 (completes SOE and his "serious need" for a "long summer and fall of "*pottering*"); and 56 (Fall 1979), 331 (mentions a novel in progress, SL, his teaching schedule, and more lecturing and writing).

1960

C43 "One Sunday in Late July." *Encounter*, 14 (March 1960), 13–33. Story.

The biographical note on p. 96 of this number states that a collection of Price's stories, *A Long and Happy Life*, will be published later that year by Chatto & Windus.

Fifty offprints in stapled white wrappers were prepared for private distribution by the author.

Appears in slightly revised format as the opening of **A1**.

1961

C44 "First Novelists—Summer 1961." *Library Journal*, 86 (1 June 1961). Contains Price's prepared statement on pp. 2128–29.

C45 Untitled review of James E. Miller, Jr., *Myths and Method: Modern Theories of Fiction. South Atlantic Quarterly*, 40 (Summer 1961), 373–74.

C46 "The Warrior Princess Ozimba." *Virginia Quarterly Review*, 37 (Summer 1961), 425–31. Story.

Price contributed a brief autobiographical statement which appears on p. lxxvii, in "The Green Room" section, of the *Virginia Quarterly Review*.

Rept. in **B5**; **A2**; **C52**; *Southern Writing in the Sixties: Fiction*, ed. John William Corrington and Miller Williams (Baton Rouge: Louisiana State Univ. Press, 1966), pp. 3–9; *Stories of the Modern South*, ed. Benjamin Forkner and Patrick Samway (New York: Bantam Books, 1978), pp. 293–98.

C47 "After Hölderlin." *Encounter*, 17 (Nov. 1961), 4. Poem.

1962

C48 "Uncle Grant." *Encounter*, 18 (Jan. 1962), 42–52. Story.

Rept. in **A2**; *Modern Short Stories: The Uses of the Imagination*, rev. ed., ed. Arthur Mizener (New York: W. W. Norton, 1967), pp. 692–709 (Price's story does not appear in the 1st ed., 1962, nor is it reprinted in the 3d and 4th eds., 1971 and 1979 respectively).

C49 Excerpts from a letter to *Saturday Review* staff in "Country Girl Burdened with Love." *Saturday Review*, 45 (10 March 1962), 17.

Price comments on the writing of A *Long and Happy Life*.

C50 "Winter" (after Hölderlin). *Carçanet* (Merton College, Oxford), [1] (1962), 29. Poem.

Rept. in the *Archive*, 83 (Autumn 1970), 40.

C51 "As various as roads—the lines life takes" (after Hölderlin). *Carçanet*, [1] (1962), 29. Poem.

Rept. as "The Lines of Life" in *Shenandoah*. 17 (Winter 1966), 69. Also published separately; see above **A27**.

1963

C52 "A Story and Why." *Duke Alumni Register*, 49 (April 1963), 31–35. Price discusses the writing of "The Warrior Princess Ozimba"; the story is reprinted on pp. 33–35.

C53 "Summer Games." *Vogue*, 142 (15 Aug. 1963), 89. Elegy.

In his note "To the Reader" in *Permanent Errors* (**A8**), Price describes "Summer Games" and the other story-poems included in Section Two as "elegies." These are clearly personal, he writes, "but none . . . is intended as a story—more nearly as poems; narrative poems of personal loss, therefore elegies." (Four of these elegies were first reprinted in *Love and Work* [**A5**] and labeled "poems.")
Rept. in **A8**; *The Norton Sampler: Short Essays for Composition*, ed. Thomas Cooley (New York: W. W. Norton, 1979), pp. 132–34.

C54 "The Names and Faces of Heroes." *Shenandoah*, 14 (Summer 1963), 13–41. Story.

Rept. in **A2**; *The Best American Short Stories 1964*, ed. Martha Foley and David Burnett (Cambridge: Houghton Mifflin, 1964), pp. 257–83.

1964

C55 "Clearer Road Signs in His Country." *Book Week*, 1 (12 Jan. 1964), 5. Review of Cleanth Brooks, *William Faulkner: The Yoknapatawpha Country*.

C56 "Country Mouse, City Mouse." *Book Week*, 2 (10 May 1964), 8. Essay.

Published separately; see above, **A34**.

C57 "A Cautious Cricket in the Cotton." *Book Week*, 1 (4 Oct. 1964), 4. Review of Frank E. Smith, *Congressman from Mississippi*.

C58 "Sleeping and Waking." *Shenandoah*, 16 (Autumn 1964), 38–40. Story.

Rept. in **A8**.

C59 "Morning Places." *Red Clay Reader*, [1] (1964), 67–68. Story.

Rept. in **A8**.

1965

C60 "Truth and Lies." *Southern Review*, N.S. 1 (April 1965), 292–306. Story.

Rept. in **A8**.

C61 "A Long and Happy Life: Fragments of Groundwork." *Virginia Quarterly Review*, 41 (Spring 1965), 235–47. Excerpts from the notebook kept by Price while studying at Oxford.

Rept. in **B7**.

C62 "Our Own Heart of Darkness." *Book Week*, 2 (1 Aug. 1965), 4. Review of *Mississippi Black Paper* and Sally Belfrage, *Freedom Summer*.

1966

C63 "A Question of Influence." *New York Times Book Review*, 29 May 1966, pp. 2, 12–13. Essay.

Rept. separately with authorial revisions as *The Thing Itself*; see above, **A4**.

C64 "Reborn to light this day in late July". *Shenandoah*, 17 (Summer 1966), 6–7. Poem.

This poem, written in collaboration with Wallace Kaufman, is addressed to Rosacoke Mustian's unborn child and is printed with the Kaufman interview also contained in this issue. The poem, and an expanded version of the interview, is reprinted in *Kite-Flying and Other Irrational Acts: Conversations with Twelve Southern Writers*, ed. John Carr (Baton Rouge: Louisiana State Univ. Press, 1972); see below, **E36**.

C65 "Life for Life." *Esquire*, 66 (Dec. 1966), 246. Poem.

Rept., with several authorial changes, in **A6**, **A8**, and **B13**.

C66 "The Sleeper in the Valley" (after Rimbaud). *Shenandoah*, 17 (Winter 1966), 69. Poem.

1967

C67 "Brave New World." *Book Week*, 4 (12 Feb. 1967), 8. Review of John T. Scopes and James Presley, *Center of the Storm*.

C68 "Finding Work." *Chanticleer* (Duke Univ. yearbook), 55 ([June] 1967), 8–22. Essay.

C69 "Invitation (for Jessie Rehder 1908–1967)." *Shenandoah*, 19 (Aug. 1967), 37–39. Story.

Rept. in **A8**.

1968

C70 "A Dog's Death." *Southern Review*, N.S. 5 (Spring 1968), 392–95. Story.

Rept. in **A8**.

C71 "*Pylon*, The Posture of Worship." *Shenandoah*, 19 (Spring 1968), 392–95. Story.

Rept. in **B8**, **A8**.

C72 "The Knowledge of My Mother's Coming Death." *Southern Review*, N.S. 4 (Summer 1968), 720–24. Elegy.

Rept. in **A6**; **A8**, and *A Duke Miscellany: Narrative and Verse of the Sixties*, ed. William Blackburn (Durham: Duke Univ. Press, 1970), pp. 224–27.

C73 "News for the Mineshaft." *Virginia Quarterly Review*, 44 (Autumn 1968), 641–58. Essay.

Price discusses the writing and critical reception of *A Generous Man*. Rept. in **B9**, **A10**.

C74 "Scars." *Esquire*, 70 (Dec. 1968), 184–85, 272–73, 275–76, 278–80. Story.

Rept. in **A8**.

1969

C75 "Man and Faun" (after Stefan George, *Der Mensch und der Drud*). *Carolina Quarterly*, 21 (Spring 1969), 17–19. Poem.

Rept. in **B12**, **A36**.

C76 "The Onlooker Smiling: An Early Reading of *The Optimist's Daughter*." *Shenandoah*, 20 (Spring 1969), 58–73. Essay-review of Eudora Welty, *The Optimist's Daughter*.

Rept. in **A10**.

C77 "Why Think of College at All? Why Duke?" *Bulletin of Duke University* (Information for Prospective Students), 41 (June 1969), 7–16. Essay.

This essay has since been reprinted annually, with minor revisions, in the *Bulletin*.

C78 "Life in the Deep South." *North Carolina Anvil*, 3 (5 July 1969), 1. Review of Anthony Dunbar, *The Will to Survive*.

C79 "The Happiness of Others." *Southern Review*, N.S. 5 (Oct. 1969), 1176–82. Story.

Rept. in **A8**.

1970

C80 "Frightening Gift." *Washington Post*, 17 April 1970, p. 1(C). Review of Eudora Welty, *Losing Battles*.

Rept. in **A10**.

C81 "Waiting at Dachau." *Esquire*, 72 (April 1970), 130–33, 186–92. Story.

Rept. in **A8**; *Prize Stories 1971: The O. Henry Awards*, ed. William Abrahams (Garden City, N.Y.: Doubleday, 1971), pp. 67–93; and, with a long note by Price, **B15**.

C82 "Good Dreams, Bad Dreams." *Playboy*, 17 (May 1970), 133, 210–13. Story.

Rept. as "Good and Bad Dreams" in **A8**.

C83 "Two Versions from the Bible" (Genesis 22:1–14, and John 8:48–59). *Shenandoah*, 21 (Spring 1970), 150–51.

"Genesis 22:1–14" rept. in slightly revised version in **C90**, pp. 151–52.

C84 "Five Versions." *Archive*, 83 (Autumn 1970), 40–42. Poems. The five versions are "Black Water" (after a German folk song), "Winter" (after Hölderlin), "Midnight" (after Goethe), "Half of Life" (after Hölderlin), and "Initiation" (after Rilke).

1971

C85 "Walker Percy in the Ruins." *Chicago Daily News*, 15–16 May 1971, "Panorama" section, p. 7. Review of Walker Percy, *Love in the Ruins*.

C86 "Poem Doctrinal and Exemplary to a Nation: A Reading of *Samson Agonistes*." *Shenandoah*, 23 (Fall 1971), 3–36. Essay.

Rept. in **A10**.

C87 Untitled statement used as a preface. *Winged Words* 1971 (Broughton High School, Raleigh, N.C., student literary magazine), p. [6].

"Twenty years ago *Winged Words* made some of my early prose and verse available to my fellow students at Broughton. The work was not as good as it might have been, even at the time (not as attentive or clearsighted or ruthless-to-self); and seeing it duplicated on page after page, hearing it read and discussed by my friends and teachers, I came to see some of those weaknesses sooner than I might have done if I'd gone on cherishing my bejewelled babies in a drawer at home. So I remember the magazine and its first editors, Mary Forrest and Blair Jenkins, with real gratitude and affection; and I wish its present and future incarnations many more decades of life and high standards."

1972

C88 "Epistolary Epic." *Washington Post*, 28 April 1972, pp. 1, 10(B). Review of Robert Manson Myers, *Children of Pride*.

Rept. in part in *Book-of-the-Month-Club News*, January 1973, but Price's name was accidentally dropped, thus the republication is unsigned.

C89 "For Ernest Hemingway." *New American Review*, 14 (April 1972), 38–66. Essay.

Offprints of this essay were prepared by the publisher, stapled in light grayish-blue printed wrappers.
Rept. in A10.

C90 "Four Abrahams, Four Isaacs by Rembrandt (notes before a novel)." *Prose*, 4 (Spring 1972), 151–60. "Four Abrahams" is a reprinting with minor authorial revisions of "Genesis 22:1–14" (C83), and "Four Isaacs by Rembrandt" gives Price's impressions of three etchings and an oil by the Dutch master.

Rept. in A10.

C91 "Seven Poems about Death." *Shenandoah*, 23 (Summer 1972), 74–75. The seven poems are "After a Haiku of Basho"; "Remembering Golden Bells" (after Po Chü-I / Waley), and "Five Epitaphs from the Greek Anthology": "after Plato, Book VII, 704"; "Anonymous, Book 7, 704"; "Damascius the Philosopher, Book VII, 553"; "Anonymous, Book VII, 324"; and "Callimachus, Book VII, 453."

C92 "To My Niece: Our Photograph, in a Hammock." *Southern Review*, N.S. 8 (Autumn 1972), 912–13. Poem.

Rept. in slightly different version in A20; B22.

C93 "Dodging Apples." *South Atlantic Quarterly*, 71 (Winter 1972), 1–15. Essay about the creative process in general and the creation of "Michael Egerton" in particular.

Rept. in A10; *South Atlantic Quarterly*, 76 (1977), 518–32.

C94 "Mentor of Authors Succumbs at Duke." *Durham Morning Herald*, 10 Dec. 1972, p. 1(A). Article about William Blackburn which includes a prepared statement by Price.

1973

C95 Letter to the editor on the Bollingen Prize. *New York Times*, 19 Feb. 1973, Sec. 1, p. 22.

Price is writing in response to the *Times* editorial of 16 January "which deplores the academic grip on the Bollingen Prize for Poetry." Price suggests that the actual effect of the piece in the *Times* is the "denigration" of the work of James Merrill, the winner.

C96 "The Heart in Dreams." *Esquire*, 79 (April 1973), 75–82, 180–204. Excerpt from SOE (in progress).

Price's poem, "To Hades As You Enter His Door: To Be Placed in Your Hand," is first printed on p. 194 of this issue of *Esquire*, and is represented on p. 43 of **A15**.

C97 "At the Gulf." *American Review*, 17 (May 1973), 148–50. Poem.

Two wrappers have been noted (priority undetermined): (1) bright, tannish brown front and rear wraps and spine; (2) duller tannish brown front and rear wraps and a light gray spine. The differences are distinct and were not created by age or sunning.
    Rept. in **A20**.

C98 "One Time, One Place." *Bulletin of the Southern Heritage Society*, July 1973, 3–4. Review announcing the July selection, Eudora Welty's *One Time, One Place*.

C99 "What Did Emma Bovary Do in Bed?" *Esquire*, 80 (Aug. 1973), 80, 144–46. Essay.

C100 "England's Largest Living Novelist." *New York Times Book Review*, 9 Sept. 1973, 1, 18, 20. Review of Graham Greene, *The Honorary Consul* and *Collected Stories*.

Excerpt rept. In *Modern British Literature*, IV (Supplement), comp. and ed. by Martin Tucker and Rita Stein (New York: Frederick Ungar, 1975), pp. 175–76.

C101 "Genesis 15, Deuteronomy 32." *St. Andrews Review* (St. Andrews Presbyterian College, Laurinburg, N.C., student literary magazine), 2 (Fall/Winter 1973), 210. Translations.

Rept. in slightly different versions in **A22**.

C102 "Why Think of College?" *New York Times*, 7 Oct. 1973, Sec. 11, p. 12. Essay.

This is a reworking of **C77** and **E70**.

C103 Untitled introduction for William Blackburn, "Sketches for a Memoir." *Duke Alumni Register*, 59 (Winter 1973), 18.

1974

C104   "Intruder in the Dust." *Washington Post Book World*, 1 (10 March 1974), p. 1. Review of Joseph Blotner, *Faulkner: A Biography.*

Rept. in the *Chronicle* (Duke Univ. student newspaper), 28 March 1974, as "Faulkner: Lacking the 'Unexplored Silence.'"

C105   "Something Ended." *Southern Voices*, 1 (March/April 1974), 17–22. Excerpt from SOE (in progress).

C106   "Dry-spiritedness." *Chronicle* (Duke Univ.), 4 April 1974, p. 7. Letter.

Price defends "the entirely serious and illuminating image of the supernatural" in the film version of William Blatty's *The Exorcist*. The letter was written in response to a review in the 26 March issue and is signed "Yours in the battered but perennial hope of responsible criticism, Reynolds Price, Department of English."

C107   "Night and Day at Panacea." *Harper's Magazine*, 249 (Aug. 1974), 70–76. Excerpt from SOE (in progress).

Rept. In *The Best American Short Stories 1975*, ed. Martha Foley (Boston: Houghton Mifflin, 1975), pp. 197–211.

C108   "When Is an Indian Novel Not an Indian Novel?" *New York Times Book Review*, 10 Nov. 1974, p. 1. Review of James Welch, *Winter in the Blood.*

1975

C109   "Honest Hearts." *Esquire*, 83 (March 1975), 98–103, 134–40. Excerpt from SOE (in progress).

C110   "Commencing." *Virginia Quarterly Review*, 51 (Spring 1975), 282–93. Excerpt from SOE (in progress).

C111   "Neglected Books of the Twentieth Century: Part Two." *Antaeus*, 19 (Autumn 1975), 136–40. Price's contribution is found on p. 140; he mentions James Salter, *A Sport and a Pastime*; Romulus Linney, *Slowly, by Thy Hand Unfurled*; and Fred Chappell, *It Is Time, Lord.*

C112   "Mr. Death." *New York Times Book Review*, 16 Nov. 1975, p. 32. Review of Anne Moody, *Mr. Death: Four Stories.*

C113 "Broad Day." *Shenandoah*, 26 (Winter 1975), 7–17. Excerpt from SOE (in progress).

Rept. in *The Best American Short Stories 1976*, ed. Martha Foley (Boston: Houghton Mifflin, 1976), pp. 209–19.

1976

C114 "A Daughter's Memories." *New York Times Book Review*, 14 March 1976, pp. 7–8. Review of Lucille Clifton, *Generations: A Memoir*.

C115 "God Bless the Child Who Reads." *Esquire*, 85 (March 1976), 94, 129–30. Essay which includes a list of Price's favorite childhood books.

Rept. in the *Duke Alumni Register*, August 1976, under Price's original title, "You Are Needed Now and Will Always Be," pp. 12–14, with two illustrations, one a photograph of Price as a child and one an illustration from a childhood Bible story book of Price's.

C116 "Papa." *New York Times Book Review*, 30 May 1976, pp. 1–2. Review of Gregory H. Hemingway, *Papa: A Personal Memoir*.

C117 "Three Versions of Two Poems by Michelangelo." *Archive*, 88 (Spring 1976), 12–13. The poems are "In Me Death" (two versions) and "I Am Transmuting."

C118 "Given Time: Beginning *The Surface of Earth*." *Antaeus*, 21/22 (Spring/Summer 1976), 57–64. Essay containing excerpts from the working notes for SOE.

C119 "Works in Progress." *North Carolina Anvil*, 10 (21 Oct. 1976), 8. Includes Price's statement on *A Palpable God* (in progress).

"I'm working on a book of translations of short narratives from the Old and New Testaments. I have long been interested in the structure and tradition of the narrative form, so I've been looking back at the beginnings of narrative in western civilization. And to study them closely—since contemporary translations are nearly paraphrases—I've needed to translate those parts of the Bible which interest me. I will be writing an essay as preface to the book, and I am also doing some heavy reading."

1977

C120 "Family Stories: The Carters in Plains." *Time*, 3 Jan. 1977, pp. 26, 29. Essay. See also **C131, C140**.

C121 "The South: A Proud Moment." *Washington Post,* 20 Jan. 1977, Special Inauguration Section, pp. 1, 14–15. Essay.

The paragraphs in this essay were inadvertently printed out of sequence.

C122 "God and Man in Louisiana." *Washington Post Book World,* 27 Feb. 1977, p. 7. Review of Walker Percy, *Lancelot.*

C123 "Homecountry, East Texas." *New York Times Book Review,* 22 May 1977, p. 7. Review of William Humphrey, *Farther Off from Heaven.*

C124 "Two Years Underway: Pages from a Notebook." *Archive,* 89 (Spring 1977), 7–17. Excerpts from a notebook kept by Price during the period just before he left for Oxford (1955) and during the period of his study there. Included are notes for the story which became "The Anniversary."

C125 "Black Family Chronicle." *New York Times Book Review,* 11 Sept. 1977, pp. 1, 48, 50. Review of Toni Morrison, *Song of Solomon.*

C126 "Home: An American Obsession." *Saturday Review,* 5 (26 Nov. 1977), 9–16. Essay.

Rept. In the Raleigh *News and Observer,* 1 Jan. 1978, Sec. IV, p. 1, and in the *Charlotte Observer,* 8 Jan. 1978, "Perspective" section, p. 1.

1978

C127 "Talk with Eudora Welty." *New York Times Book Review,* 7 May 1978, pp. 7, 42–43. Article based on an interview with Welty, on the occasion of the publication of her *The Eye of the Story.*

C128 "The Heroes of Our Times." *Saturday Review,* 5 (Dec. 1978), 16–17. Essay.

C129 Unsigned citation accompanying Hiro photograph of Leontyne Price. *Saturday Review,* 5 (Dec. 1978), 20.

1979

C130 "Naked Boy." *Carolina Quarterly,* 31 (Winter 1979), 13–16. Poem.

Rept. in **A36.**

C131 "The Strong Old Rhythm of Plains." *Time,* 113 (5 Feb. 1979), 14–15, 17. See also **C120, C140.**

C132 "The First Printing of 'Place in Fiction.'" *Eudora Welty Newsletter,* 3 (April 1979), 6–7. Essay. See above, **C33.**

C133 "According to Lattimore." *New York Times Book Review,* 15 April 1979, pp. 1, 24. Essay-review of Richmond Lattimore, *The Four Gospels and the Revelation.*

C134 "Two Sorrowful Mysteries, One Joyous." *Ontario Review,* 10 (Spring-Summer 1979), 49–56. Poems.

Rept. in **A29; A36.**

C135 "The Dream of Lee." *Massachusetts Review,* 20 (Autumn 1979), 468–71. Poem.

Rept. in **A36.**

C136 "Gertrude Merritt." *Duke University Library Newsletter,* N.S. 23 (Oct. 1979), 4. An appreciation by Price.

C137 "A Normal Year." *New York Times Book Review,* 4 Nov. 1979, pp. 14, 49. Essay-review of *The Best American Short Stories 1979.*

C138 "The Annual Heron." *Poetry,* 135 (Dec. 1979), 154–60. Poem.

Published separately as **A31;** rept. in **A36.**

C139 "Oh, Cuisine!" *Saturday Review,* 29 Dec. 1979, 54. Essay in which Price discusses his idea of a southern "Platonic restaurant."

1980

C140 "The Collected Stories of Eudora Welty." *New Republic,* 31 (1 Nov. 1980), 31–34. Review.

C141 "In Georgia: Plains Revisited." *Time* ("American Scene" sect.), 22 Dec. 1980, 5–6. Essay. See above, **C120, C131.**

1981

C142 "Benediction." *Antaeus,* no. 40/41 (Winter-Spring 1981), 166–75. Excerpt from SL (in progress).

Issued in cloth with dust jacket and in printed pictorial wrappers.

C143 "The Art of American Short Stories." *New York Times Book Review,* 1 March 1981, pp. 1, 20. Review of Mark Helprin, *Ellis Island,* and *The Stories of Elizabeth Spencer.*

C144 "In Search of Adult Love." *New York Times Book Review,* 24 May 1981, p. 5. Review of Francine du Plessix Gray, *World without End.*

C145 "Rescue." *Poetry,* 138 (June 1981), 144–48. Poem.

Rept. in **A36.**

C146 "K. A. Porter: A Self-Portrait in Soft Focus." *Chicago Tribune Bookworld,* 12 July 1981, p. 4. Review of Enrique Hank Lopez, *Conversations with Katherine Anne Porter.*

C147 "The Bible Tells Me So." *Washington Post Book World,* 30 Aug. 1981, p. 4. Review of Robert Alter, *The Art of Biblical Narrative.*

1982

C148 "Letter to a Young Writer." *Writers Forum,* 8 (1982), i–v. Preface to this issue.

C149 "Sacred and Profane Love." *Washington Post Book World,* 7 Feb. 1982, pp. 1, 2. Review of Robertson Davies, *The Rebel Angels.*

C150 "The Road to Devotion." *New York Times Book Review,* 11 April 1982, pp. 12, 28. Review of Frederick Buechner, *The Sacred Journey.*

C151 "Love across the Lines." *South Atlantic Review,* 47 (May 1982), 1–11. Essay.

C152 "Pritchett's Small Treasures Radiate a Cold, Satirical Light" *Chicago Tribune Book World,* 23 May 1982, pp. 1, 6. Review of V. S. Pritchett, *Collected Stories.*

C153 "Seafarer" (after the Anglo-Saxon). *Ontario Review*, 16 (Spring-Summer 1982), 20–22. Poem.

Rept. in **A36**.

C154 "Pictures of the Dead." *Poetry*, 140 (Aug. 1982), 258–60. Poem in three parts: "1. Robert Frost, 1951"; "2. W. H. Auden, 1957"; "3. Robert Lowell, 1968."

Rept. in **A36**.

C155 "Bethlehem—Cave of the Nativity," and "Jerusalem—Calvary." *Southern Review*, N.S. 18 (Summer 1982), 534–35. Poems.

Rept. in **A36**.

C156 "Women's Voices." *Dial*, 3 (Sept. 1982), 34–35. Essay.

C157 "Divine Propositions." *Georgia Review*, 36 (Fall 1982), 638. Poem.

Rept. in **A36**.

C158 "Farewell with Photographs." *Atlanta*, 22 (Dec. 1982), 89. Poem.

C159 "Searching for Saint Paul." *Washington Post Book World*, 26 Dec. 1982, pp. 1, 14. Review of Richmond Lattimore, *Acts and Letters of the Apostles*.

1983

C160 "Southern Journal: Penny Show." *Southern Living*, March 1983, 112. Essay.

C161 "Ambrosia." *Poetry*, 143 (Nov. 1983), 90–92. Poem.

1984

C162 "A Heaven for Elizabeth Rodwell, My Mother." *Poetry*, 144 (June 1984), 144–48. Poem.

C163 "Porta Nigra (after Hölderlin)." *Ontario Review*, 20 (Spring-Summer 1984), 89. Poem.

C164 "House Snake." *TriQuarterly*, no. 61 (Fall 1984), 15–26. Poem.

C165 "Rincón: The Strangers." *New Yorker*, 60 (24 Dec. 1984), 34. Poem.

D

Translations

A Long and Happy Life

D1   *Kilden i skovens dyb.* Copenhagen: Steen Hasselbalchs Forlag, 1962. 212 pp. Trans. Adolf Hallman. Wrappers with jacket.

D2   *Onnea ja pitkää ikää.* Helsinki: Kustannusosakeyhtiö Tammi, 1963. 208 pp. Trans. Ritva Tiusanen. Paper-covered boards, red imitation leather spine, with jacket.

D3   *Et langt og lykkelig liv.* Oslo: Gyldendal Norsk Forlag, 1963. 220 pp. Trans. Finn Aasen. Clothbound with jacket; also wrappers with jacket.

D4   *Ett långt och lyckligt liv.* Stockholm: Wahlström & Widstrand, 1963. 192 pp. Trans. Lily Vallquist. Clothbound with jacket; also wrappers with jacket.

D5   *Une vie longue et heureuse.* Paris: Editions Stock, 1963. 224 pp. Trans. Lucile Veyrier. Wrappers.

D6   *Una Lunga Vita Felice.* Milan: Bompiani, 1963. 232 pp. Trans. Giancarlo Bonacina. Pictorial paper-covered boards; heavy glassine jacket printed in black and white.

D7   *Ein langes glückliches Leben.* Frankfurt am Main: Surhkamp Verlag, 1963. 256 pp. Trans. Margaret Sander. Clothbound with jacket. Surhkamp also published a second edition in 1965. 212 pp. Wrappers.

D8   *Ein langes glückliches Leben.* Darmstadt: Dt. Buch-Gemeinschaft, 1964. 261 pp. Trans. Margaret Sander. Not seen.

D9   *Długie lata szczęścia.* Warsaw: Czytelnik, 1964. 208 pp. Trans. Ariadna Demkowska-Bohdziewicz. Wrappers with jacket.

D10   *Długie lata szczęścia.* Warsaw: Ksiazka i Wiedza, 1975. 248 pp. Trans. Ariadna Demkowska-Bohdziewicz. Wrappers.

D11   *Gia Mia Zoe Eutuchismene.* Athens: Phethes, 1965. 172 pp. Trans. Paulou Nathanael. Wrappers.

D12   *Una Vida Larga y Feliz.* Buenos Aires: Editorial Sudamericana, 1969. 236 pp. Trans. Roberto Bixio. Wrappers.

D13   *Itsumademo Shiawase Ni.* Tokyo: Fuzambo, 1970. iv, 300 pp. Trans. Tokunaga Shozo. Wrappers with jacket.

D14 *Dolgaja i Scastlivaja Zizn.* Moscow: Progress, 1971. 175 pp. Trans. N. Treneva. Not seen.

The Names and Faces of Heroes

D15 *Les noms et visages de héros.* Paris: Gallimard, 1965. 208 pp. Trans. Maurice-Edgar Coindreau. Wrappers with flaps. Has erratum slip for p. 78.

D16 *Siegerehrung für Verlierer.* Frankfurt am Main: Insel Verlag, 1971. 192 pp. Trans. Christa Monks. Clothbound with jacket.

A Generous Man

D17 *Ein ganzer Mann.* Frankfurt am Main: Insel Verlag, 1967. 276 pp. Trans. Maria Carlsson. Clothbound with jacket.

D18 *Un homme magnanime.* Paris: Gallimard, 1970. ii, 302 pp. Trans. Yvonne Davet. Wrappers with flaps.

Love and Work

D19 *Liefde op Papier.* Amsterdam: Elsevier, 1969. 152 pp. Trans. A. Pleiter. Wrappers.

Translations in newspapers and periodicals

D20 LHL was serialized in *Frankfurter Allgemeine Zeitung* from 13 Feb. to 29 Mar. 1963. Trans. Margaret Sander. Not seen.

D21 "La princesse guerrière Ozimba." *Mercure de France,* January 1965, pp. 22–29. Translation of "The Warrior Princess Ozimba" by Maurice-Edgar Coindreau.

D22 "Le Sommeil, L'Eveil." *La nouvelle revue française,* 1 Oct. 1968, pp. 480–83. Translation of "Sleeping and Waking" by Michel Gresset.

E

Interviews,

Published Discussions,

and Published Comments

1956

E1   David Murray, "Reynolds Price." Raleigh, N.C., *News and Observer*, 22 July 1956, Sec. 1, p. 17. Article.

Includes Price's comments (through letters to his mother) on his studies at Oxford and three photographs by Price.

1958

E2   Bill Strawn, "Book to Be Published: Rhodes Scholar Price Returns to Duke as University Teacher." *Winston-Salem* (N.C.) *Journal*, 24 Nov. 1958, p. 13. Article.

Includes Price's comments on Oxford, English and American universities and students, and a forthcoming book of "Southern stories" which Strawn reports will be published by Random House and Chatto and Windus in the spring of 1959.

1959

E3   Cindy Smith, "Spender Dislikes Communist Method." *Duke Chronicle*, 54 (18 May 1959), 1, 3. Article.

Includes Price's facetious remarks on Stephen Spender's one-time, short-lived membership in the Communist party. To Spender's comment that Auden influenced his life more than anyone else, then Eliot, Price interrupts: "Yes, but wasn't that the book that you burned all the copies?"

1961

E4   Nancy Mason, "Price Stresses Familiarity of Locale." *Duke Chronicle*, 10 Feb. 1961, p. 4. Article.

Includes Price's paraphrased comments on his relation to his fictional characters and how very few women writers have created credible male characters.

1962

E5   "A Sweet South Wind." *About Town* (London), 3 (Feb. 1962), "Town Talk Section," p. 4. Interview.

Topics include Price's home in North Carolina, his family, growing up with black playmates, and the lack of bitter racial prejudice in rural North Carolina.

E6   W. J. Weatherby, "You Can Go Home Again." Manchester *Guardian*, 19 April 1962, p. 9. Article.

Includes Price's comments on critics, Oxford students, the race situation in the South ("It is hard to flush it out of your blood sometimes."), southern writers coming "from a family tradition that is almost Jewish in its intensity," Sillitoe, "family" in England and in the South, himself as "an old-fashioned romantic," opposition to "the new criticism," Tolstoy, plans for future work (stories and a novel "about a boy and his father who drinks"), Fred Coe and the proposed film version of LHL ("That book still means a lot to me and I wouldn't want it done wrong by."), and his feeling that "I think I'll live in North Carolina all my life."

E7   Maurice Dolbier, "Books and Authors" (column). *New York Herald Tribune*, 3 June 1962, Sec. 6 ("Books"), p. 2. Article.

Includes Price's comments on the proposed film version of LHL, "a sense of place" as one of a novelist's greatest strengths, and his writing habits.

E8   Lewis Nichols, "In and Out of Books" (column). *New York Times Book Review*, 3 June 1962, p. 8. Brief article based on a conversation with Price.

Topics include LHL, NFH (forthcoming), and his fictional characters.

E9   Jonathan Friendly, "The Fast and Happy Rise of Reynolds Price." Raleigh *News and Observer*, 22 July 1962, Sec. 3, p. 3. Interview.

Topics include LHL, Price's southern middle-class characters, Faulkner, Price's admiration of Tolstoy, and his plans for a film version of LHL.

E10   "Betty Hodges' Book Nook" (column). *Durham* (N.C.) *Morning Herald*, 9 Sept. 1962, p. 5(D). Article based on a conversation with Price.

Topics include his writing habits ("definitely longhand—very longhand," he comments), LHL, "A Chain of Love," the South, and reading.

E11   Garry Blanchard, "Price Isn't Faulkner—Just from the Same Seed." *Charlotte* (N.C.) *Observer*, 9 Dec. 1962, p. 5(H). Interview.

Topics include LHL, the South, Price's family, the oral tradition in the South, Faulkner, teaching, writing habits, and reading.

E12 J. A. C. Dunn, "A Talk with Reynolds Price." *Chapel Hill Weekly*, 23 Dec. 1962, pp. 1, 8. Interview.

Topics include NFH (in progress), Price's writing habits, his interest in what he is writing more than in what he has written, critical expectations of second books, John O'Hara, John Updike, Kafka, Conrad, Faulkner, Tolstoy, teaching, student writing, Katherine Anne Porter, and other women writers.

1963

E13 "Interview with Reynolds Price." *Rebel* (East Carolina College [University], Greenville, N.C., student literary magazine), 6 (Winter 1963), 4–9.

Topics include Price's growing up in eastern North Carolina, his future writing plans, North Carolina as the scene of his fiction, LHL, English and American literary life and criticism, critics in general, teaching as "a form of priesthood," American writers in the university, teaching writing and the importance of writing courses to aspiring young writers, the relative difficulty in "comparing" writers (past and present), Walker Percy's *The Movie-Goer* [sic], Faulkner and Thomas Wolfe, the "articulateness" of southerners on all levels of society, Styron's *Lie Down in Darkness*, his techniques of writing, his conscious effort to make his fiction "readable," "unreadable" fiction such as *Finnegans Wake*, and his selectivity of detail.

E14 Ed Rowland, "Price, Audience Enjoy [Eudora Welty's] Visit." *Raleigh* (N.C.) *Times*, 19 April 1963, p. 1. Article.

Included are Price's comments on the "mystery" of making a work of art, the "why" of writing, and his reasons for writing.

E15 Harriet Doar, "His 'Act of Faith' Won Prizes." *Charlotte Observer*, 24 April 1963, p. 13(A). Article.

Includes Price's comments on male-created female characters, man's better understanding of woman (and his own character, Rosacoke Mustian), the South and Faulkner, the "why" of art as more important than the "how," and his own reasons for writing.

E16 Harriet Doar, "Of Saints and Tin Ears." *Charlotte Observer*, 28 April 1963, p. 5(C). Article.

Includes Price's comments to an informal gathering of students at Davidson College.

E17 "Arts Aim Viewed by Reynolds Price." *Chapel Hill Weekly*, 28 April 1963, p. 5(B). Article.

Includes Price's comments on the importance of the "why" of art, the mysterious nature of creation in art, and his own writing as a means to better understanding of the "mysterious."

E18 W. H. Scarborough, "Price Is for People: The Evolution of Writing." *Chapel Hill Weekly*, 14 July 1963, p. 3(B). Article.

Includes Price's comments on Faulkner and the differences in their writing, "Uncle Grant," the importance of the right title for a story, reading, and sources of ideas in his fiction writing.

E19 Joe Goodman, "Author Dislikes Writing." *Winston-Salem Journal*, 31 July 1963, p. 5. Interview.

Topics include Price's writing habits, Eudora Welty, and his purpose in writing.

E20 "Speakers at the Denver Dinner." *Publishers' Weekly*, 18 Nov. 1963, p. 13. Notice.

Price is quoted: "The richest, wisest, most nearly complete fiction of the next 20 years will be regional."

E21 "Wednesday Club Hears Price on Writing Novels." *Danville* (Va.) *Bee*, 12 Dec. 1963, p. 2. Article.

Includes Price's paraphrased comments on his reasons for writing, his belief that "all works of art exist for a kinetic purpose, or to cause movement, action, or work some change," and his own writing as "historical fiction," not autobiography.

1964

E22 Peter Bart, "Young Novelists Turning to Films: Author of A Long and Happy Life to Do Screenplay." *New York Times*, 26 Dec. 1964, p. 8. Article.

Quotes Price on films: "While the previous generation of writers looked upon films with contempt, I think that my contemporaries instinctively think in cinematic terms." Price continues: "We are drawn to this field not only because of its familiarity, but also because the most interesting works of art of our generation have been in the realm of motion pictures."

1965

E23 Betty Bressler, "Reynolds Price to Be Discussion Panel Member." *Durham* (N.C.) *Sun*, 11 Jan. 1965, p. 7(A). Article based on an interview with Price.

Includes his comments on the movie version of LHL and Hollywood.

E24 "Betty Hodges' Book Nook." *Durham Morning Herald*, 26 Jan. 1965, p. 3(D). Article about a Price lecture, "Women by Men, Men by Women—Gender in Fiction."

Includes Price's paraphrased comments on the two sexes as they portray each other in fiction.

E25 Perry Young, "A Talk with UNC's New Writer-in-Residence: Everybody Gets Tired of Faulkner's Long Shadow." *Chapel Hill Weekly*, 21 Feb. 1965, Sec. 2, pp. 1, 8. Article.

Includes Price's comments on teaching; the differences in students from school to school; topics included (and not included) in his students' writing; his belief that students, in general, are not as "indifferent" as others say they are; President Kennedy's death and its effect on Price's writing; the genesis of GM (in progress under the working title *Clear Day*); writing the film script for LHL; his opinion that "films are potentially the most interesting of all art forms and [that] . . . most good writers would leap at the chance to write films for serious and imaginative producers"; his home and family in Warren County, N.C.; his characters, especially "Uncle Grant," who was based on a black man who lived with his family; "writing from experience"; eastern North Carolina as a setting for his work, but not the exclusive setting; southern writers "cursed" by the shadow of Faulkner's genius; how his sometimes complicated sentences reflect "very complicated emotional reality"; and his own book reviews.

E26 Eugene Moore, "In 'Isolation,' Reynolds Price Escapes Pitfalls of Success." *Atlanta Journal/Constitution*, 25 Dec. 1965, p. 15. Article.

Includes Price's comments on the forthcoming GM, New York (two weekends "gave me a bellyful of the literary circuits"), the importance of "solitude" to his work, and the comfortable isolation he enjoys in North Carolina.

1966

E27 Sam Ragan, "Southern Accent" (column). Raleigh *News and Observer*, 2 Jan. 1966, Sec. 3, p. 3. Article.

Includes Price's comments on the preoccupation with family in modern southern writing and the Negro as "a constant moral fact of life" in the South.

Ragan writes that this particular column is based on an interview with Price by Eugene Moore that had appeared "recently" in the *Atlanta Journal*. An examination of the *Journal* issues of November and December 1965 reveals only an article by Moore (see **E26**) which does not contain Price's comments on the family in modern southern writing and the Negro.

E28 Wes Lawrence, "JFK Assassination Triggers Reynolds Price into Action." Cleveland, Ohio, *Plain Dealer*, 27 March 1966, p. 7(H). Article.

Included is Price's description of how the Kennedy assassination provided the impetus for writing GM.

E29 Phyllis Méras, "Talk with Reynolds Price." *New York Times Book Review*, 27 March 1966, p. 44. Interview.

Topics include GM, the nonautobiographical nature of his writing, and GM as "a somber comedy."

E30 Harriet Doar, "I Do Work That Occurs to Me—Reynolds Price." *Charlotte Observer*, 10 April 1966, p. 1(F). Interview.

Topics include GM, the seriocomic nature of Price's work, NFH, reading, Eudora Welty, critics, and heroes in literature.

E31 Eugene Moore, "Price's Second Novel Splendid." *Atlanta Journal/Constitution*, 10 April 1966, p. 2(B). Book review of GM.

Includes Price's paraphrased comment to Moore that, in his personal opinion, GM "outreaches" LHL.

E32 Harriet Doar, "Writers and Readers: Man to Watch." *Charlotte Observer*, 17 April 1966, p. 6(F). Article.

Price comments briefly on the proposed film version of LHL.

E33 "Betty Hodges' Book Nook." *Durham Morning Herald*, 8 May 1966, p. 5(D). Article based on a conversation with Price.

Includes Price's comments on Faulkner and other southern writers ("they imitate *their* South as Faulkner imitated his South"), the importance of Eudora Welty to his work, the "instant" as the poet's subject and "years" as the novelist's, literature that has influenced him, and his indebtedness to the various members of his family.

E34 "Work and Play." *New York Times Book Review* (Vacation Issue), 5 June 1966, pp. 1, 60–62. "A pride of literary lions was asked, 'What will you do with your leisure this summer, if you have any?'" Price's response is on p. 61.

E35 "It's Leisure Writing Time." *Charlotte Observer*, 12 June 1966, p. 1(G). Article concerning the way certain North Carolina writers plan to spend the summer.

Price, who is staying at home to write short stories and "whatever unplanned chooses to surface," comments: "If nothing should [surface] I'll slouch around my house and woods, staring at the small pond beneath my window and what surfaces there."

E36 Wallace Kaufman, "A Conversation with Reynolds Price." *Shenandoah*, 17 (Summer 1966), 3–25. Interview.

Topics include Price's poetry translating, his relationship with and debt to other southern writers (especially Eudora Welty), the South as his home, LHL, GM, NFH, symbols in his writing, his characters, ghosts and the supernatural (particularly as they relate to GM), comedy as "a function of experience . . .[and] life," urbanization of the United States, Price's prose style, "pop culture" of the 1960s, his childhood, likes and dislikes in art and music, the relationship of the writer to his surroundings, L&W, Milton and Tolstoy as the writers Price most admires, the Bible as literature, and his future.

Brief excerpts from this interview are included in "Betty Hodges' Book Nook," *Durham Morning Herald*, 25 Sept. 1966, p. 5(D), and a longer excerpt is in the *North Carolina Anvil*, 1 (1 June 1968), 8.

E37 Porter Carswell, Jr., "A Short and Happy Visit: An Interview with Reynolds Price." *Savannah Morning News / Savannah Evening Press Magazine*, 18 Dec. 1966, p. 3. Article.

Price tells an amusing story about his flight to Savannah.

E38 Eugene Moore, "On Writing, Readers, Critics." *Red Clay Reader*, 3 (1966), 18–26. Interview.

Topics include LHL, GM, the lack of commitment in the writing of many 20th-century novelists, Price's writing habits, Vermeer's *The Letter* as the inspiration for the idea which became LHL, teaching, reading, hostile critics, southern writing and the "oral culture" of the South, his personal desire to make his readers "see" not "feel," satisfaction in his work, and his desire to write a play.

E39 Grayce Northcross, "A Visit with a Young Writer." *America Illustrated* (Russian language edition), 116 [1966], 24–26. Interview.

Topics include teaching, Price's students in particular and young people in general, the South, his lifelong interest in the arts, his high school English teacher (Phyllis Peacock) and her influence on him, William Blackburn, Eudora Welty, JFK's assassination as the event that triggered the writing of GM, his writing habits, his success, and writing as "an attempt to understand the life of the spirit."

A photocopy of a typescript translation of this interview is located in the Manuscript Department of the Perkins Library, Duke University.

1967

E40 "Betty Hodges' Book Nook." *Durham Morning Herald,* 26 March 1967, p. 5(D). Article on "The Writer's Role" sponsored by the annual North Carolina Literary Forum in Raleigh.

Price is quoted as saying that he would like to substitute "duty" for "role" and that he wants to write things that are "beautiful or memorable" in a style that is clear and comprehensible.

E41 *The Arts & The Public,* ed. James E. Miller, Jr., and Paul D. Herring (Chicago and London: Univ. of Chicago Press, 1967). Published discussion (Price, Wayne Booth, Wright Morris, Richard Stern, Theodore Solotaroff, Leon Edel, Hoke Norris, James E. Miller, Jr., Granville Hicks, Anthony West, Edward W. Rosenheim, Jr., Harold Rosenberg, Katherine Kuh, and Harry Bouras). Major topic is contemporary fiction; Price's comments are included on pp. 230–31, 237, 240–41, and 246–47.

1968

E42 Bonnie Aikman, "A New Literary Reality?" Washington, D.C., *Sunday Star,* "Washington Book Notes" section, 10 March 1968, p. 8. Article based on a discussion held at the Library of Congress after a reading by Price and John Cheever; James Dickey moderated.

Includes Price's comment on "the strong sense of [the] supernatural" that pervades Cheever's fiction.

E43 "Betty Hodges' Book Nook." *Durham Morning Herald,* 12 May 1968, p. 5(D). Article about an autographing party for Price.

Includes his comments on his published books to date, especially L&W, and his remarks to student autograph hunters.

E44 "A Question of Commitment." *New York Times Book Review* (Summer Reading Issue), 2 June 1968, pp. 2–3, 14. Authors tell how they are going to spend the summer. Price's comments are included on p. 3.

E45 "Betty Hodges' Book Nook." *Durham Morning Herald*, 16 June 1968, p. 5(D). Article based on a conversation with Price.

Includes his comments on the revived interest in a film version of LHL and his personal belief in the film as an art form.

E46 "An Evening with Reynolds Price." *Duke Chronicle*, 5 Nov. 1968, p. 10. Article.

Includes a few brief comments by Price on writing.

1969

E47 "Profile of Reynolds Price." *Druid* (University of Tennessee [Knoxville] student literary magazine), May 1969, pp. 2–5, 26. Interview.

Topics include the generation gap, the Vietnam War, the necessarily demanding nature of writing, Price's translating ("impersonating") poetry to understand it better, his early desire to be an artist, "inspiration," his writing "schedule," the role of the Negro in southern writing, and American industrial society.

E48 "The Professional Viewpoint." *20th Century Studies* (University of Kent), 2 (Nov. 1969), 109–30. Price's comments on the treatment of sexual themes in the modern novel are found on pp. 122–23. Contributors include, among others, Anthony Burgess, Pamela Hansford Johnson, Jack Kerouac, James Purdy, John Updike, and John Wain.

1970

E49 June Lioret, "Novelist, Teacher, Southerner . . . Reynolds Price Now Has Five Books to His Credit." *Raleigh Times*, 26 Sept. 1970, p. 18. Interview.

Topics include PE, Oxford, teaching, his writing habits, and his success as a writer.

E50 Untitled interview. *Brogue* (Belhaven College, Jackson, Miss., student literary magazine), 2 [1970], 25–33.

Topics include reading, the difficulties young writers have getting published, the "how" of writing, the importance of daily writing for the novelist, his own writing habits, southern writers in general, and Eudora Welty in particular.

"The fourth issue of *Brogue* is respectfully dedicated to Mr. Reynolds Price in recognition of his literary achievements and in gratitude for his kind permission to print his interview at Belhaven."

1971

E51 Rod Cockshutt, "A Glimpse into the Very Private World of a Novelist." Raleigh *News and Observer*, 24 Jan. 1971, Sec. 4, p. 3. Interview.

Topics include living alone, Price's family, his childhood, books and authors he reads and likes, Hemingway, Faulkner, Welty, the "mystique of the Southern writer," and his writing habits.

E52 Bill Neal, "Reynolds Price: Writer-in-Residence." *Duke Chronicle*, 12 March 1971, p. 5. Interview (first part; see **E53** for second part).

Topics include Price's Milton course at Duke, W. H. Auden, difficulties involved in writing, his characters, PE, writing habits, and the "movie" idea of a writer such as that portrayed by Dr. Zhivago.

E53 Bill Neal, "Price–II." *Duke Chronicle*, 15 March 1971, p. 4. Interview (second part).

Topics include southern writers, tradition, Price's own South, Faulkner, Welty and her influence on his writing, Flannery O'Connor, Price's juvenilia, William Blackburn, "Michael Egerton," and "A Chain of Love."

1972

E54 "An Interview with Reynolds Price." *Ariel* (Washington and Lee University student literary magazine), 10 (Winter 1972), 3–17.

Topics include LHL, the mobility of American society, Tom Wolfe, the novel as a "retrospective form" communication and "parajournalism," writing out of compulsion rather then desire, his poetry and translations, contemporary poetry, novelists he respects as writers, the success of LHL and his recent work, GM, his interest in writing for the movies, "urban" critics and southern writing, Eudora Welty's novels, critics and criticism in general, teaching, and *King Lear*.

E55 "William Blackburn: Teacher of Writers." *Furman Magazine* (Furman University, Greenville, S.C., alumni magazine), 19

(Spring 1972), 23–29. Contains a long statement by Price on pp. 28–29.

E56 "Betty Hodges' Book Nook." *Durham Morning Herald*, 16 April 1972, p. 5(D). Article based on a conversation with Price.

Includes his comments on TT, PE, paperback books (which, he comments, have "a very subtle and insidious effect on young people especially"), and the general loss of respect for books as important objects.

E57 Dot Jackson, "Sex in Novel Has Limits, Author Says." *Charlotte Observer*, 28 Oct. 1972, pp. 1, 6(C). Article.

Includes Price's comments on the distinction between novelists and "pornographers," *Madame Bovary*, Tolstoy, and sex as a topic in the novel.

E58 "Betty Hodges' Book Nook." *Durham Morning Herald*, 24 Dec. 1972, p. 5(D). Article.

Includes Price's comments on William Blackburn.

1974

E59 Dan Benyon, "Poem Makes Debut at Gilmer Talk." *Savannah Morning News*, 3 May 1974, p. 1(D). Article.

Includes Price's comments on writing poetry and his translations and on the Bible, which, he says, exemplifies the "oldest and most successful" form of narration.

1975

E60 John Stevenson, "Price Completes Long Process of Creation." *Duke Chronicle*, 9 April 1975, p. 12. Article.

Includes Price's comments on the nearly completed SOE and its background and SOE as a "complex" novel.

E61 Harriet Doar, "Price's Novel Embraces Armful of Years." *Charlotte Observer*, 20 July 1975, p. 4(B). Interview.

Topics include SOE, family and time, growing up in a story-telling family, the narrative form, growing up with blacks, male guilt over childbirth in the pre-1940s generations, and Price's personal pleasure with SOE.

E62 Gustav Magrinat, "Again, a Changing South; the Dimming of Values Reflected by Reynolds Price." *Greensboro Daily News*, 20 July 1975, p. 1(B). Interview.

Topics include the South and its past, the idea of family, LHL, NFH, L&W, GM, PE, SOE, and race.

E63 Howard Kissel, "The South as Seen by Native Son." *Women's Wear Daily*, 23 July 1975, p. 14. Interview.

Topics include the southern literary tradition, the importance of reading a good novel "closely," SOE, the lack of stability in American society, and Price's reason for writing (his body "secretes narrative prose").

E64 John F. Baker, "Reynolds Price." *Publishers' Weekly*, 208 (4 Aug. 1975), 12–13. Interview.

Topics include Oxford, LHL, SOE, southern writers and their world, Tolstoy, Hardy, and Chekhov, critics in general, and the critical reception of SOE.

E65 Jim Clark, "Reynolds Price—An Interview." *Greensboro Sun*, 20 Aug. 1975, pp. 8, 11.

Topics include Price's reading habits (while he is writing), the critical reception of SOE, the novel as a literary form, the South and the revival of interest in the South, theology, "story-telling" as an important element in his writing, and sources for SOE.

E66 Lindsay Miller, "Reynolds Price." *New York Post Magazine*, 6 Sept. 1975, "Book and Author" column, p. 15. Article.

Includes his comments on nightmares and the subconscious, the relative ease with which he wrote SOE, man-woman relationships three decades ago, and his insistence that he is not a Freudian ("I do not analyze. I simply describe.").

1976

E67 Gail Jensen, "'Why Duke?'—An Update." *Duke Chronicle*, 21 Feb. 1976, p. 12. Excerpts from an interview with Price, presented as an update and sequel to his article "Why think of college at all?" See C80 and C105.

E68 Val Lauder, "Reynolds Price on Narrative: From Beowulf to Bunker." Raleigh *News and Observer*, 11 April 1976, Sec. IV, p. 7. Article.

Includes Price's comments on the narrative form, reading, the oral tradition, TV as "wonderful company," the film version of *Gone with the Wind* ("It's the best story, almost the best story, I can think of."), creativity and writing, the importance of "memory" in writing fiction, teaching, and the durability of first-class fiction.

E69   William Ray, "Conversations." *Bulletin of the Mississippi Valley Collection* (Memphis State University), 9 (Fall 1976), entire issue.

Topics include L&W, PE, GM, TT, SOE, rural North Carolina as a backdrop for his fiction, Price's family, his childhood, the South and southern writers, teaching, the oral tradition, the abuse and decline of the spoken language, Welty, Agee, Updike, Roth, William Faulkner as a language "*reminder*" (not as a model), writers and books Price admires, the craft of writing, rural southern English as a "language of vision," writing habits, the importance of "family" in his works, race relations, Eros as a great force in his life, the names of his characters, and his ideas of "novelistic excellence." This issue of the *Bulletin* consists of 500 copies.

E70   "Works in Progress. . . ." *North Carolina Anvil*, 10 (21 Oct. 1976), 8–9. Contains brief statements from North Carolina poets and novelists about works in progress. Price's statement is included on p. 8.

E71   William Greider, "Politics as Bad Fiction." *Washington Post*, 15 Nov. 1976, p. 8. Article.

Includes Price's comments on the desouthernization of President Carter ("he's beginning to look dangerously ordinary," Price concludes).

E72   Georges Gary, "A Great Deal More." *Recherches Anglaises et Américaines*, 9 (1976), 135–54. Interview.

Topics include Price's student years at Duke, teaching, the Vietnam era, his view of the South in vertical rather than horizontal divisions, his poetry, the role of the novelist, his years in England (and Europe), "plantation novels," his childhood relation to blacks, "Night and Day at Panacea," Eudora Welty and other contemporary writers he reads, detective fiction as a genre, preference for the rural South as his home, writing habits, the importance of humor, critics, "News for the Mineshaft," the literary marketplace, certain of his characters, his own past as a source of material, and religion. A limited number of offprints stapled in printed wrappers were prepared.

1977

E73   R. Granville Coleman, "North Carolina's Noted Novelist Reynolds Price Likes Bible Stories, and He Thinks He Can Make Them More Interesting by Rewriting Them." *People of North Carolina*, Sept. 1977, p. 32. Article.

Includes Price's comments on the difficulty of getting first novels published, Bible stories as the oldest and most successful form of narrative, and his personal interest in these stories and in translating them.

E74 Mark Kirby, "Students' Creativity Not in 'Golden Period': Trinity Writing Fizzles." *Duke Chronicle*, 7 Oct. 1977, p. 1. Article.

Includes Price's paraphrased comments on the downward trend in student writing (not just at Duke but nationwide).

1978

E75 Ann J. Abadie, "University Symposium Honors Eudora Welty." *Ole Miss Alumni Review*, 27 (Spring 1978), 8–10. Article.

Includes Price's comments on Welty's work on p. 9.

E76 Sam Ragan, "Southern Accent" (column). Southern Pines, N.C., *Pilot* 4 Oct. 1978, p. 1(B). Article.

Contains Price's paraphrased comments on novel writing: he does not make notes, knows what the ending will be, and likes to let his characters live their own story. "I love to create characters," Price states.

E77 "William Blackburn and His Pupils: A Conversation." *Mississippi Quarterly*, 31 (Fall 1978), 605–14. Published transcription of a conversation among Blackburn, Price, William Styron, Mac Hyman, and Fred Chappell; the conversation was originally recorded on 3 Feb. 1963 for the ABC radio and television program "Meet the Professor."

Topics include the training and encouragement of young writers, the influence that an established writer can have over a beginner, the importance of experience and maturity to the young writer, the effect of a college creative-writing program on an aspiring author, and the idea that most writers have been lonely as youths.

E78 Constance Rooke, "On Women and His Own Work: An Interview with Reynolds Price." *Southern Review*, N.S. 14 (Oct. 1978), 706–25.

Topics include the theme of love in Price's work, Christian elements in his writing, the basically comic nature of his work, the central characters in L&W and the near impossibility of "married love" in American society today, his books as books about "human freedom," and Price's view of himself as a "truth-sayer" rather than a "yea- or nay-sayer."

1979

E79 "Carter and Country." *Bill Moyers' Journal*, 12 Feb. 1979. Photocopied transcript. 13 leaves; text on rectos and versos; rectos

and versos paginated [i–ii], 1–24; the 13 leaves are stapled together in the upper left-hand corner. In addition to Price, partic-
ipants in this discussion were Brooks Holifield, Nicholas von
Hoffman, Charles Hamilton, James Fallows, and Bill Miller.
Price's comments are found on pp. 6, 7, 8, 9, 10, 13, 14, 17,
22, and 23.

E80   "The Creative Process: The Novel." *North Carolina Historical
       Review*, 56 (Spring 1979), 206–8. Edited transcript of remarks
       made by Price at a meeting of the North Carolina Literary and
       Historical Association.

E81   Betty Hodges, "With Reynolds Price: 'Joyful, Sorrowful, Glo-
       rious' Poems Are Byproduct of Work." *Durham Morning Her-
       ald*, "Book Nook" (column), 1 April 1979, p. 3(D). Article.

Includes Price's comments on translating, PG, the narrative form, his childhood interest in Bible stories, and seven recent poems based on New Testament narratives, of which he says: "In writing the poems I realized it is
quite possible to view both the Old and the New Testaments as love stories.
In the Old Testament God falls in love with a man called Abraham and in
the New Testament God falls in love with Jesus."

E82   Dannye Romine, "Reynolds Price: 'A Time, A Place, A Quota'
       His Formula." *Charlotte Observer*, "Carolina Writers" (column),
       15 July 1979, pp. 1, 5(F). Article based on a conversation with
       Price.

Includes Price's comments on his recent visit and interview with Eudora
Welty, the comparative loneliness of contemporary life as contrasted to the
"spiritual supermarket" available to youths of his generation (through the
presence of older people), his view that "evil is stupid and uninteresting and
simple-minded," his writing habits and the "unconscious," and his advice
to his own students: "Don't write about people you wouldn't want to watch
through a keyhole. If you don't want to spend an hour with them, why
spend a week writing about them."

E83   Paul Binding, *Separate Country: A Literary Journey through the
       American South* (New York & London: Paddington Press Ltd.,
       [August] 1979). Includes a chapter, "Reynolds Price," pp. 182–
       97, which reprints excerpts from Price's fiction and from selected
       interviews and also includes his comments on the South and
       southerners from an interview with Binding here first published.

E84   William W. Starr, "Reynolds Price: The Southern Writer Who
       Objects to Being Labeled a Southern Writer." Columbia, S.C.
       State Magazine, 9 Sept. 1979, pp. 20–21. Interview.

Includes Price's comments on being a southern writer and the general "antagonism" toward things southern; critics and their "lamentable taste for novelty" in fiction; Jewish writers and writing; writers who have helped and encouraged him (Welty and Spender); the role of the literary editor; certain of his characters, including Rosacoke Mustian, as stemming from his early school years in Warren County, N.C.; his reading habits; and his love of opera and music.

E85   "Bible Translations Clear Way for Novel." *Duke Alumni Register*, 66 (Sept.–Oct. 1979), 8. Article-review of A *Palpable God*.

Contains an excerpt from Price's introduction and includes his comments on the translations.

E86   Robin Byrd, "Beneath the Surface of Reynolds Price." *Student* (Wake Forest University student literary magazine), Fall 1979, 10–16. Interview.

Topics include Price's female characters, his novel in progress (as yet untitled), "urban critics," regional writing, translations of his novels into other languages, the comic elements in his fiction, his current interest in writing poetry and a forthcoming volume of his poems (*Nine Mysteries*), his reading habits, the American family, changes in the South, southern blacks, the use of dialects in his writing, American publishing today, his interest in art and music, and his childhood home in North Carolina.

E87   Kevin Nance, "Duke Grad Makes Film." *Chronicle* (Duke Univ. student newspaper), 22 Oct. 1979, p. 1. Article.

Includes Price's comments on two former Duke students who wrote, directed, and produced the film *Agee: A Sovereign Prince of the English Language*.

E88   Carolyn Mitchell, "Author Offers Insight to Play." *Chattanooga Times*, 28 Nov. 1979, p. 4. Article based on an interview.

Includes Price's comments on a University of Tennessee at Chattanooga production of his play *Early Dark*.

1980

E89   Jackie Young, "Modern Day Martin Luther?" *Leader* (Research Triangle, N.C., weekly newspaper). 8 May 1980, p. 15. Article.

Includes Price's comments on his biblical translations, the sequel to *SOE* (forthcoming), *PG*, and *Nine Mysteries*.

E90 Michiko Kakutani, "Portrait of the Artist as a First Novelist." *New York Times Book Review,* 8 June 1980, pp. 7, 38–39. Article.

Contains on p. 39 Price's comments on the proliferation of college writing programs.

1981

E91 Barbara Boughton, "Storytellers." *Greensboro Daily News,* 11 Jan. 1981, pp. 1, 3(D). Article based on an interview.

Includes Price's comments on his childhoood in Warren County, N.C.; his student years at Duke Univ.; writing stories ("A story is spontaneous. It just sort of dawns on you. It fills up your mind, like a dream does at night, or is drained out of you."); his pastimes ("movies, travel, eating too much"); and his fictional characters.

E92 Phyllis Tyler, "A Generous Teacher." *Spectator* (Raleigh, N.C.), 9 April 1981, p. 7(C). Article based on an interview.

Includes Price's paraphrased comments on his work and characters. (Phyllis Tyler is the mother of author Anne Tyler.)

E93 William W. Starr, "Reynolds Price." *State* (Columbia, S.C.), 19 April 1981, p. 10(B). Article based on an interview.

Includes Price's comments on his fictional characters in SOE, his feeling of being done with his Kendall and Mayfield characters after SL, and his father's death.

E94 Chris Handal, "Reynolds Price Exemplifies South's Quality." *Gamecock* (Univ. of South Carolina, Columbia, student newspaper), 22 April 1981, p. 10. Article.

Includes Price's comments on President Reagan's budget cuts for the NEA, detective fiction, and teaching at Duke.

E95 Rod Cockshutt, "A Conversation with Reynolds Price." *Tarheel: The Magazine of North Carolina,* 9 (May 1981), 28–29.

Topics include his family background, childhood reading, SL, writing habits, keeping a journal, his fictional characters, why he lives where he lives, critics, and his PBS play, "Private Contentment."

E96 Chris Tucker, "Writer Just Can't Shed His 'Southern' Roots." *Dallas Morning News,* 7 May 1981, p. 10(C). Article based on an interview.

Includes Price's comments on being a southerner, William Faulkner, his attachment to places, "extended families," and themes in his work.

E97 Bryan Woolley, "Reynolds Price No Twig Cut from Faulkner's Tree." *Dallas Times Herald,* 17 May 1981, p. 4(P). Article based on an interview.

Includes Price's comments on the fact that he is unlike and not influenced by Faulkner; the feeling that some outsiders have that southerners are "foreigners"; writing on the Carters in Plains, Ga.; SOE and SL; and the "restlessness" of contemporary Americans.

E98 Leslie Hanscom, "Story-Telling Power in an Ample Southern Voice." *Newsday,* 7 June 1981, p. 18. Article based on an interview.

Includes Price's comments on Faulkner and Hemingway, teaching at Duke, his family, and contemporary "experimental" writers.

E99 Eve Oakley, "Reynolds Price: Hot Stuff Again." *Fayetteville* (N.C.) *Times,* 12 July 1981, p. 1(G). Article based on an interview.

Includes Price's comments on SL, writers and writing, today's youth, detective fiction, writing on deadlines, and his critical success as a writer.

E100 Joyce Leviton, "North Carolina's Terry Sanford Goes Dukes Up to Get a Nixon Library." *People,* 28 Sept. 1981, p. 83. Article.

Includes Price's comment: "If you tore down every building in Europe that bears the name of a morally reprehensible person, it would be a bare scene."

E101 Shirley Williams, "Novelist Reynolds Price Believes Writers Have to Find Their Pace." *Courier Journal* (Louisville, Ky.), 9 Nov. 1981, p. 5(B). Article based on an interview.

Includes Price's comments on his writing habits; his PBS play, "Private Contentment"; Anne Tyler; the idea of family; his reading; *Anna Karenina*; and drawing as a hobby.

1982

E102 George Witte, "The Enduring Identity of Literature in the South." *Aeolus* (weekly magazine of the Duke Univ. *Chronicle*), 17 Feb. 1982, pp. 6–7. Article.

Includes Price's comment on "Southern" writing: "Literature which purposefully manipulates the 'Southern' stereotypes is almost always bad," whereas fine southern writing is "simply good work which is conditioned by the region and environment of a particular author."

E103 "The Price We Play." *CenterPiece* (Univ. of N.C. Center for Public TV, monthly magazine), April 1982, pp. 3–4. Interview.

Includes Price's comments on the North Carolina background of his PBS play, "Private Contentment"; Eudora Welty; his childhood; life in the forties and fifties; and enjoyment of seeing his work on the screen.

E104 Sarah Carey, "Writers: How to Survive Your Own Literary Career." *Florida Flambeau*, 69 (6 April 1982), 10. Article.

Includes Price's comments from a symposium on "Writing and Surviving."

E105 "Price Makes Debut as a Screenwriter." *Durham Sun*, 22 April 1982, p. 12(D). Article about Price's PBS play, "Private Contentment."

Includes his comments on the background of the play, which he calls a "comic mystery" based on a childhood fantasy.

E106 Jim Wise, "Novelist Price Has TV Debut with PBS Play." *T. V. World: April 25–May 1 1982 (Durham Morning Herald* weekly supplement), pp. 1, 12(F). Article.

Includes Price's comment on the PBS production of "Private Contentment": "They've done a beautiful job."

E107 Dannye Romine, "What Some Carolina Writers Are Reading." *Charlotte Observer*, 22 Aug. 1982, p. 6(F). Article.

Price states that he is "reading myself" in galleys and proof.

E108 Jerry Dean, "'Southern' Pigeonhole Causes Author to Squirm." *Arkansas Gazette* (Little Rock), 30 Oct. 1982, pp. 1, 10(B). Article based on an interview.

Includes Price's comments on southern writers and writing; his childhood and literary influences; and how difficult it is nowadays for young writers to get published.

1983

E109 William W. Starr, "Reynolds Price Speaks on Poetic Imagination." *State* (Columbia, S.C.), 30 Jan. 1983, p. 10(G). Article based on an interview.

Includes Price's comments on writing poetry.

E110 Ursula Werner, "Artists in Academia: Creative Professors." *Chronicle*, 25 March 1983, pp. 6–7, 14. Article.

Includes Price's comments on teaching and writing.

E111 Daniel Voll, "The Spy That Stayed: A Conversation with Reynolds Price." *Tobacco Road* (Durham, N.C.), April 1983, pp. 4–6.

Topics include Duke students, teaching and the university system, the innocence of today's students, sexual liberation, American vs. European education, teaching at Duke, the movies, writing habits, LHL, and Eudora Welty.

E112 Allison Adams, "Price Sheds Light on 'Early Dark.'" *Durham Sun*, 20 Oct. 1983, Sec. D, pp. 1–2. Interview.

Discussion of the production of the play.

E113 "Casting Light on 'Early Dark.'" *Chronicle*, 27 Oct. 1983, p. 3. Interview.

Price and director John Clum discuss the play with Allen W. Hubsch.

E114 Terry Roberts, "Love and Work: The Art of Reynolds Price." *Arts Journal* (Asheville, N.C.), 8 (Sept. 1983), 6–10. Interview.

Topics include work in progress, LHL, writing habits, and southern writers and writing.

F

Miscellaneous

F1 "I summon you to life mysterious." *Alice Tully Hall Program*, 1969–70, p. A. Price's translation of a portion of Alexander Scriabin's "Le Poème de l'Extase" for inclusion in the program for the Voytek Matushevski recital, 25 Feb. 1970. Matushevski played Scriabin's Sonata No. 5, Op. 53.

F2 Untitled statement by Price concerning the Atlantic Center for the Arts, New Smyrna Beach, Fla., 1982. Contained on the recto of a flyer soliciting applicants for the 3-week session beginning 1 Nov. 1982. Price, Edward Albee, and Mia Westerlund Roosen were the artists-in-residence for the session.

Index